PRISONER OF THE MOUND BUILDERS

PRISONER OF THE MOUND BUILDERS

LLOYD HARNISHFEGER

Illustrated by
GEORGE OVERLIE

Published by
Lerner Publications Company
Minneapolis, Minnesota

BOOKS BY LLOYD HARNISHFEGER

Prisoner of the Mound Builders
Hunters of the Black Swamp

International Standard Book Number: 0-8225-0754-4
Library of Congress Catalog Card Number: 72-7655

CONTENTS

CHAPTER 1

O-Tah-Wah the Hunter

The elk bounded away over the thick grass, clearing every obstacle without breaking stride. Its great, dark head was held low, the jaw thrust straight forward, allowing the antlers to lie neatly along its back. Just before the bull reached the top of the hill, two cows broke cover on the far side of the meadow, and all three sprinted up the rise and disappeared.

O-Tah-Wah was furious. This was the third time in four days that he had stalked the elk within bowshot, only to see them bolt in panic just as he was ready to fire off an arrow. What was wrong with the game here? He was beginning to fear this rolling, hilly country.

In a fit of rage, the young man kicked viciously at the bushes with his good leg. This did not help anything at all, but only made a tear in his doeskin leggings that would take several hours to mend. Sullenly, O-Tah-Wah glared down at his ugly, misshapen right leg. As usual, he blamed his bad luck on the stiff limb that had been his misfortune since birth. "Probably," he thought angrily, "the foolish thing brushed against a twig or scraped a rock. It is always the way with such a Lazy One!" He called the bad right leg "Lazy One," for it would neither bend at the knee nor do its fair share in the work of walking.

O-Tah-Wah was not being truthful with himself, however. He knew that no sound had alerted the elk at all. Something was strange and different in this part of the forest, so far to the south from his usual hunting grounds.

For many days, O-Tah-Wah had been working his way farther and farther from his village. And as he did so, he had become uneasy at the signs he was reading. Small birds, for example, were often quite tame near his home. But here, they fluttered away in fright as soon as the hunter came near. Game was scarce, too, although there seemed to be plenty of grass and water everywhere. The young hunter would have left the area four days before, had he not struck the elks' trail and stayed on it.

O-Tah-Wah was nervous as well as angry. He eased his body into an awkward sitting position, the hated Lazy One jutting out at its usual unnatural angle. When O-Tah-Wah's anger had cooled enough for clear thinking, the lad carefully retied the knot of black hair that was always arranged in a neat coil at the base of his skull.

Next he pulled his otter-skin quiver around to the front of his body and drew out one long heavy arrow. For many moments he sat, holding the crude weapon in one hand and turning it slowly between thumb and finger. Making up his mind at last, O-Tah-Wah yanked a tiny piece of fluff from the feathered shaft and stood up. Holding the pinch of down in one hand, he raised it high above his head. With eyes tightly closed, he let go and waited. When he was sure that enough time had passed, he opened his eyes and quickly began searching for the small brownish tuft. O-Tah-Wah felt a moment of panic when it did not readily come into view. But after a few frantic minutes, he found it, clinging to a wild strawberry leaf an inch from the ground. Eagerly, he snatched it up. The feather had not touched the earth! This sign meant that it would be safe and wise to follow the elk herd even farther, if necessary, into this strange land. O-Tah-Wah was thankful that old Kinawee, his grandfather, had taught him such ways to determine whether his luck would be good or bad. O-Tah-Wah could not imagine what he would do in a situation like this one if he had not been instructed in the reading of signs and omens.

The hunter rose to his feet with confidence. While still a boy, he had decided that what the bad leg could not help the good leg do, the good leg would have to do alone. O-Tah-Wah was a young man now, and the rest of his body was hard and strong. The muscles in his back and neck rippled under his smoky-colored skin like otters playing in a deep pool.

Parting the bushes behind which he had been hiding, O-Tah-Wah broke into the peculiar loping trot he had taught himself to use when he needed to travel faster. Near the crown of the hill, he slowed to a walk and began taking advantage of any small trees and bushes that could help cover his approach. It was just possible that the elk had stopped running on the other slope. If so, there might still be a chance to stalk them until they were within range of his bow.

The last few yards took several minutes of silent creeping. This maneuver was doubly hard for the crippled hunter. The way he had learned to crawl was as clever as it was difficult. The Lazy One was thrown over the good left leg, and it simply rode along, out of the way.

O-Tah-Wah crept under a low-lying bush and rested for several moments until his breathing was back to normal. Then he silently drew an arrow from his quiver and fitted it to the short stiff bow that never left his hand on a hunt. Wriggling noiselessly forward, he finally parted the bushes and looked into the valley beyond him.

The scene spread out below was a very strange one for this man from the flat country to the north. Below and to his left was a large ugly hill of earth. Brush and trees had been cleared away from the structure for a good distance on all sides. It stood silent and strange, looking raw and out of place among the beautiful, tree-lined hills nearby.

A movement in the forest directly below caught O-Tah-Wah's eye, and he stopped breathing, freezing his body as if it were one of the stones upon which he lay. The elk were forgotten completely now. The hunter knew that he was in very great danger. Everything he saw told him what in his foolishness he had done. O-Tah-Wah had blundered into the land of the Mound Builders!

How well his own tribe, several days' journey to the north, had known of these terrible people and their bloody practices. They worshipped strange gods and kept humans for slaves. O-Tah-Wah flattened his body even more, attempting to melt into the very earth itself. He kept his eyes glued to the clump of trees below, hardly knowing what to expect.

Gradually, he began to see them. There were many men working in the grove. Even from this distance, the hunter could tell that they were going about the business of burning down trees. What amazed him, however, was the number of workers. There were at least twice as many workers as O-Tah-Wah had fingers and toes. In fact, more grown men could be seen in the grove than were in O-Tah-Wah's entire village!

Bitterly, the hunter's thoughts turned once again to the Lazy One. Had it not been for the stiff leg, he wouldn't be here all alone in this dangerous position. O-Tah-Wah's tribe had not really chased him away, but he had tired of their constant taunts and teasing. Each year, as he came nearer to manhood, O-Tah-Wah had spent more and more time alone. And each year, he had ranged ever farther across the hills and rivers of the area that one day would be called the Ohio Country. His body had been toughened by the cold winter and the driving rains that came with the spring. He had learned many things from being alone, and he was fast becoming a fine, skillful hunter. It had been almost a full month since he had last seen his people. The moving figures below were proof enough, however, that this time he had traveled too far.

O-Tah-Wah knew that he must plan quickly now. These people were without doubt the Mound Builders. How they would enjoy catching a strange young tribesman alone within their own hunting grounds! The young man's heart pounded painfully as he recalled the terrifying tales his grandfather had told of the wicked priests and cruel chiefs who ruled the great empire that sprawled in all directions outward from its center near the Beautiful River. Many were the cold nights O-Tah-Wah had lain under his feather robes, listening to stories of men who left camp, never to return. Their fate had been capture and enslavement by the Mound Builders!

Though very frightened, O-Tah-Wah was thinking hard as he watched the distant workers going about their tasks below him. With growing dread, O-Tah-Wah noticed that these figures did their work in a chilling silence. Had this been a scene in almost any of the villages with which he was familiar, there would have been shouting and laughter as the trees were prepared for felling. Realizing what this silence must mean, O-Tah-Wah worked harder than ever on a plan for escape.

The problem, he knew, was his back trail. In swift pursuit of the elk band, he had foolishly paid no attention to his own footprints. Any hunter who chanced to cross them would be certain to notice the trail, especially since the Lazy One's dragging shuffle left a track that the smallest child in his village could have followed with ease. Yes, O-Tah-Wah knew that the greater danger did not lie in front of him; these men were busy at their work. It was from the rear that the worst threat came.

Several plans entered O-Tah-Wah's head and were rejected almost as soon as they were formed. Backtracking and using a leafy branch to blot out his own trail would be too noisy. Also, he would be forced to cross the open meadow again if he backtracked. Traveling *around* the open meadow would not be wise, either, for this might take him near a camp or village, where the dogs would certainly catch his scent and lead the entire band straight to him.

Finally, O-Tah-Wah decided that his best chance for escape would be to lie where he was until nightfall. Then he would head back along his own trail, being sure to destroy his tracks as he went. It would be very difficult at night, but once across the open areas, he felt that he could once again travel fast toward the north. If he was discovered before the darkness came, O-Tah-Wah assured himself that he would fight, even though he knew it would be impossible to hold out for long. Better death, he decided, than capture and torture—or slavery!

Since it was only midmorning, O-Tah-Wah knew that he must spend many long hours in this very spot, waiting for the rise of the evening star. Even though the summer was nearing its end, the day was hot. Insects hummed lazily among the leaves and flowers within the tiny thicket where the silent hunter lay. By cautiously raising his head above the bushes, O-Tah-Wah was able to observe the workers below. And with each look, he became less frightened. The workers were obviously unaware of him, and it seemed unlikely that they would soon leave the grove in which they were working. O-Tah-Wah's fear subsided slowly as he noticed these things, and soon he felt safe enough to allow himself to doze off for a few minutes at a time.

The hunter was very tired, and hungry, having traveled hard for three days on almost no rations. But now he was glad that his hunger had not been satisfied earlier, for he realized that had he been able to put an arrow into the elk, the Mound Builders would most certainly have discovered him. The desire for sleep grew stronger, and O-Tah-Wah told himself that he would need rest for the coming night. Checking the arrow in his bowstring, he curled his left forefinger over it while the rest of his hand gripped the bow. He propped two more arrows carefully across a low bush so that their feathered ends were close at hand. If he were discovered, the readied arrows would allow him three quick shots, after which he would run to new cover before shooting again.

O-Tah-Wah's fighting axe made a hard pillow, but the tired hunter placed its polished ash handle under his cheek and soon fell asleep. The sun climbed higher and higher into a cloudless blue sky as the young hunter slept soundly under the leafy cover of the small thicket. He was unaware of the two little boys who were playing at hunting near the workmen in the grove.

The two young hunters were very excited, and they had reason to be, for they had just discovered the elks' trail! Quickly, they decided not to tell the men, even though they knew they were supposed to. They would track the animals themselves. This they proceeded to do, not realizing that they were following the trail backwards.

Moving with great caution, the two young hunters crept up the steep hill toward the small clump of brush where the tracks disappeared. The small brown bodies were bent almost double as they slithered through the tall grass near the crest of the hill. Two tiny rabbit bows were drawn and ready.

The taller of the two boys entered the thicket first, crawling on hands and knees along the loose earth kicked up by the big splayed hooves being made before him. Suddenly, the first tracker stopped short, staring in surprise and fright at the sight of a strange brave lying asleep under the bushes. Turning pale with fear, the boy twisted his head around and signaled his friend to remain silent. Both boys then crept out of the thicket, taking great care to make no sound. Once out in the sunshine again, the boys began to run straight down the hillside, heading for the grove. O-Tah-Wah had been discovered.

The hunter awoke with a start, not sure what had wakened him. He quickly checked his weapons, then listened hard for sounds of danger. He could hear nothing, but still he did not relax. Something was wrong! The crickets, which should at midday be chirping with a great racket, were silent. There seemed to be no hum of bees, either. O-Tah-Wah sensed danger very strongly now. No sounds came from the grove below. Had the workers left, or had his trail been discovered? The hunter's nostrils flared wide as he tested the breeze. The muscles in his forearm and back swelled tight and hard as he lay, poised for any action he must take.

Fool! O-Tah-Wah thought angrily. How stupid not to have chosen a hiding place with a better view of his back trail. He was sure by now that someone was stalking him, but he did not wish to give his position away until he knew the strength of the enemy. Suddenly, he saw something that set his heart hammering. A pair of brown legs moving in absolute silence were in view for a moment through the leaves on his left. Hardly had this pair of legs disappeared until he saw several more legs straight ahead. Then a soft rasping sound, instantly quieted, betrayed an enemy behind him moving clumsily through the briars. O-Tah-Wah did not attempt to fool himself. He was surrounded!

The crippled hunter's fierce temper threatened to blot out his thinking ability. It was very hard for him to resist a desire to burst from his hiding place and attack his enemies. With an effort, however, he forced himself to lie still and think. Still blaming the Lazy One for his troubles, O-Tah-Wah felt certain that most of the attacking force would be located behind him, since they must have been following his trail. Therefore, he reasoned that his best chances would be ahead, down the hill. This idea was actually a mistake, of course, since the two boys had never found his trail at all but had merely stumbled onto his hiding place while tracking the elk!

O-Tah-Wah decided to make his break for freedom immediately, using the element of surprise to help him escape. He made no move to do this, however, until he had noiselessly drawn out a tiny leather pouch from inside his buckskin shirt. Suspended by a cord around his neck, the little bag contained his most powerful medicine: a tiny flake of flint, a hawk's claw, three dog's teeth, a kernel of corn, two fish bones, and two small white bones from the foot of a raccoon. There were exactly as many items as he had fingers on each hand, and O-Tah-Wah felt that he needed these things now! The pitiful handful of objects was treated with great care as O-Tah-Wah pressed each item to his wrist for strength, then to his forehead for cunning. When he had finished with the ritual, he carefully placed each piece back in the pouch. Drawing the string tight once more, O-Tah-Wah then took a pinch of earth and placed it under his tongue. He must, of course, face the possibility that he might soon be killed. If this happened, the dirt would remind the Great Spirit that O-Tah-Wah was from the earth.

Otherwise, his soul might spend eternity wandering about the heavens, searching for a home!

O-Tah-Wah replaced the two arrows in his quiver, took three great breaths, and with a shattering scream, leaped up and crashed out of the thicket. His axe was flailing the air while his left hand held the bow and its fitted arrow ready. The Mound Builders were terrified even though they had known a strange hunter was somewhere in the thicket. They yelled in confusion as their quarry hopped away with surprising speed down the hill. Near the bottom, he cut northward.

Their wits about them at last, the group gave chase, screaming and yelling with a series of sounds so horrible that O-Tah-Wah felt himself running even faster. The Lazy One, however, made him no match for the gang behind him, and very soon they were closing in.

O-Tah-Wah decided to turn and fight now, for it was plain that he would be caught before reaching the cover of the aspen grove for which he had been heading. The gasping hunter slid to a stop behind a low bush, the only cover he could find. He was just turning to shoot an arrow when a slight whistling noise caught his ear. It was to be the last sound O-Tah-Wah would hear for nearly two days. The Mound Builder war club had been thrown from nearly 20 paces, but even at that distance the heavy weapon had struck exactly on target. O-Tah-Wah fell without a sound.

CHAPTER 2

The Captive

O-Tah-Wah climbed slowly up from the darkness of sleep, puzzled by the pain in his head. At first, he could not remember anything. But little by little, the past came back to him. He recalled the band of elk that had run away. Then the picture of his capture suddenly came rushing into his brain. Terrified, he tried to leap to his feet. But this was impossible, for he now discovered that his legs were bound together!

The young Indian shook himself roughly, trying to clear away the fogginess that seemed to blind him. The movement made his head ache, but at least he could see. Quickly scanning his surroundings, O-Tah-Wah was sickened to discover that he was lying on a moldy-smelling pile of cornhusks at the bottom of a deep pit.

The hunter was surprised to learn that his hands had not been bound together by his captors. He sat up awkwardly and began to untie the cutting thongs that bound his swollen legs tightly together. His fingers had hardly touched the rawhide when a rock struck the young hunter a sharp blow in the back. Yelping in pain, O-Tah-Wah hitched his body around until he could see where the stone had come from.

Behind and above O-Tah-Wah's smelly bed of husks, a young boy sat on a mat of woven rushes. Even though the youth could not have been more than 12 or 13, O-Tah-Wah was shocked at the hideous ways in which his appearance had been altered. The boy's head was flattened at the back, so that he seemed to be all ears and forehead. On his cheeks, zigzag lines had been tattooed. These ran downward from the corner of each eye in a way that reminded O-Tah-Wah of the tear-stained faces of babies in his own village. It was the lad's earlobes, however, that were most astonishing to the prisoner. The flesh of each lobe had been slit, probably while the child was still a baby. Then the hole had been stretched and enlarged until the lobe itself made a loop more than an inch in diameter! In these loops were curious, spool-shaped objects that sparkled and shone in the morning sun. The ear spools had been smoothed and polished until the copper of which they had been made glowed like gold.

O-Tah-Wah, mouth hanging open, stared stupidly at the boy who was apparently his guard. Such wealth he could not imagine being entrusted to even one of the wise elders of his own tiny village. Nor was that all. This mere boy wore a headband studded with freshwater pearls, and across his thin, flat chest was a necklace made from a triple strand of the strangest and most beautiful shells O-Tah-Wah had ever seen.

Seemingly unconcerned about the enormous wealth he displayed, the boy stood up. Cupping his hands around his mouth, he began to shout. "*Aii*! *Aii*! *Aii*! *Aii*!" In a few moments many people began arriving. They stood on the slopes that rimmed the gully above the pit. They were Mound Builders, for all had flattened heads and many wore the gleaming ear spools. Some of the men carried weapons that were far more beautifully fashioned and decorated than anything O-Tah-Wah had ever known.

The thongs cut painfully into his legs, but O-Tah-Wah was clever enough to make no move to untie them with so many people to stop him. The young hunter looked from one face to another, fear making him tremble in spite of a great effort to appear unafraid. Nothing seemed to be happening at all, and O-Tah-Wah wondered what it was the Mound Builders were waiting for. None of their faces showed sympathy for him or for the fact that he would soon be put to a terrible death. For the most part, the Mound Builders simply looked curious. O-Tah-Wah had the feeling that these people had often seen prisoners in this pit before.

Suddenly there was a stir in the crowd of onlookers, and O-Tah-Wah heard the sound of more feet approaching. Then he saw a most curious sight. All the people who had been staring down at him turned from the pit and bent their bodies downward from the waist until they stood with heads almost lower than their bowed backs. O-Tah-Wah was so busy watching this strange behavior that he did not notice the new arrival on his left. Then a slight sound there made him turn. When O-Tah-Wah turned, he nearly cried out in terror at what he saw. A thing that seemed like a man yet had the muzzle of a wolf and the antlers of a deer stood peering down at him. Its eyes glittered cruelly behind the white, skull-like face that sat on a very human neck and shoulders.

The captive now knew that all of the frightening things his grandfather had told him about the Mound Builders by the fires of many a winter night were true. But O-Tah-Wah's grandfather had not known nearly half of the terrors these people could bring. O-Tah-Wah hardly realized what he did as one hand slowly dug through the dank pile of cornhusks and into the soil below. When he had loosened a little piece of dirt, he slowly brought it to his lips and placed it under his tongue. The young hunter then closed his eyes, sat up very straight, and prepared to wait for death with courage.

O-Tah-Wah was not surprised when he felt several pairs of strong arms dragging him to his feet. He opened his eyes to see three stout Mound Builders loosening the bonds on his legs. They then began pushing and shoving him up the steep side of the ravine toward the waiting onlookers. Climbing had always been very difficult for O-Tah-Wah because of the Lazy One. He was determined not to show his handicap, however. He tried hard to keep ahead of the men behind him, but several times he slipped and stumbled. This brought cruel laughter from his captors. When one aimed a kick at his stiff leg, O-Tah-Wah's vicious temper erupted. A film of red actually blocked his vision for a moment. A great, fierce surge of strength and power seemed to flash through his body, and he felt far superior to anyone or anything. He spun to face his tormentors, and with a snarl, attacked in fury. O-Tah-Wah had no weapon, but in his senseless rage, he did not care. The first Mound Builder was so shocked by this sudden change in the prisoner's behavior that he completely forgot the hand axe he wore at his waist. In a panic, the Mound Builder scrambled backward, trying to get away from the lashing, snarling wild man before him. A crushing blow from O-Tah-Wah's fist caught him full in the throat, just under the chin. He went down, gasping for breath. With another fearful shriek, O-Tah-Wah leaped over his body, snatching the stone axe from the fallen man's belt as he did so. The other two captors moved apart quickly, trying to confuse the charging prisoner. Still too angry to think clearly, O-Tah-

Wah threw the axe at the nearer man. It was a quick, overhand snap that his people had learned to use very successfully over the years. The action was so fast and accurate that there was no chance for escape. The blunt end of the whistling weapon struck the Mound Builder in the face. He fell to his hands and knees, blood gushing from a smashed nose. O-Tah-Wah rushed by the man, heading for the one who still remained. As O-Tah-Wah hopped past, however, the injured Mound Builder threw out one arm, grabbed the Lazy One, and hung on. O-Tah-Wah fell headlong into the pile of husks at the bottom of the pit. The guards then leaped upon him and held him until several other men slithered down the bank to help. In a few moments, they had beaten him into submission. O-Tah-Wah knew that further fighting would be useless.

As the Mound Builders dragged O-Tah-Wah up the steep sides of the pit, he noticed that the people watching seemed delighted at the show they had seen. None of them appeared to be particularly angry at him. He had provided them with quite an exhibition. The two injured Mound Builders, limping along behind, got little sympathy from the onlookers. O-Tah-Wah shuddered at the lack of tribal feeling these people seemed to have. How, he wondered, could they have possibly built such great monuments? How did they get such a wealth of precious goods? What kept them together? He was soon to find out.

They were coming into the village now—a village unlike any other O-Tah-Wah had ever seen before. The hunter gawked in open astonishment at the number and size of the round dwelling houses. As he passed an unfinished house, he could see the clever method used by the Mound Builders in its construction. Large poles had been set deep in the ground in a side circle. The tops of the poles were bent inward and tied together. Small saplings were being carefully woven in and out between the poles, making the unfinished house look much like a huge basket that had been turned upside down. The final step would be the covering of the framework with bark sheets and clay.

All of the Mound Builders' homes were made alike, and each one appeared to be large enough to house several families, which in fact they did. O-Tah-Wah could hardly help thinking of the mean little skin-and-brush tents that his people were accustomed to. There was not much comparison here! In spite of their apparent cruelty and hardness, the Mound Builders must, he thought, be people of great wisdom.

As he was prodded and yanked along, O-Tah-Wah decided to learn all he could about these People of the Beautiful River. What stories could then be told when he returned to his village! No one would laugh or taunt him about the Lazy One *then*. Even the young maidens of his tribe might take notice of him. Up to this time, none of them had.

They were marching up a slope between a double row of the large dome-shaped houses. O-Tah-Wah had been so busy staring at these that he had not looked ahead. When at last he did, he was astonished to see a large new-looking mound looming up before him. It was not as high as the first one he had seen, but on its level top was the most elegant building the young hunter could have imagined.

A temple, its walls were made entirely of logs set in the ground so close together that each one touched the next. The cracks had been carefully filled with clay, so that the building looked solid. The roof, unlike those of the houses, was also made of logs. Even though he was still some distance away, O-Tah-Wah could only marvel and wonder at the problems the Mound Builders must have had in building such a structure. The hunter's admiration for his captors continued to grow.

The little band made quite a procession, parading through the village. O-Tah-Wah limped along first, closely followed by six warriors. Next came a small crowd of men and women, some of whom had watched O-Tah-Wah's brief but spectacular attempt to escape. Last of all was a group of children. They were of all sizes and ages, but each one had the same oddly misshapen head as the boy O-Tah-Wah had first seen at the pit. Although the adult Mound Builders also had deformed skulls, theirs were not quite as noticeable as the children's due to their hair and the variety of feathers and other head ornaments worn by nearly all of them.

O-Tah-Wah was trembling with excitement and fear. A bright ribbon of blood was trickling down the curving line of his jaw. The battle had left its marks on him. Remembering the fight, O-Tah-Wah felt the anger coming on again. His breathing became faster, and his muscles tensed uncontrollably. One of the Mound Builder guards noticed the signs. He was the same one who had been felled by the thrown axe, and he had no desire to let this barbarian from the north start anything else. Moving up quickly from behind, the square-headed Mound Builder raised his war club and dealt O-Tah-Wah a stunning blow on the head.

The crippled hunter fell heavily, showers of bright lights swimming through the tears that blinded him. The kicks and blows rained upon him were hardly noticed, for he had slipped into unconsciousness for the second time in two days.

When O-Tah-Wah awoke, he was certain that he had passed into the Spirit World. The light was quite dim, and ghostly figures could be seen gliding about in the shadows. Dully, he realized that he had not been able to put any earth under his tongue before he had come here. The ground he was lying on seemed solid enough, however, so the confused hunter felt that

his spirit must have been able to find its way back to the earth somehow. Cautiously, he felt his limbs. He was surprised to find the bumps and bruises still there. It was this knowledge that made O-Tah-Wah begin to suspect that he was not dead after all.

Attracted by O-Tah-Wah's movements and the soft groaning sounds he was making as he slowly regained consciousness, several Mound Builders had gathered around him. O-Tah-Wah struggled to sit up. As he did so, the men separated and bent themselves over at the middle, just as they had done when O-Tah-Wah had been in the pit. They remained standing in this awkward position until there appeared before them that terrible-looking monster with the antlers of a deer and the jaws of a wolf! O-Tah-Wah remembered well having seen this same awful creature once before, but he could no longer remember when or where it had been. He had suffered too many head injuries!

Dressed in a beautiful robe of fur and feathers, the monster rose from his skin-covered seat and moved closer to O-Tah-Wah. O-Tah-Wah shrank back in terror as the monster approached. But suddenly, O-Tah-Wah found himself face to face with a finely dressed old man. The "monster" had removed his wolf-jaw mask and revealed himself to be the high priest Cotauna.

Cotauna, whose name meant "favored leader," was especially interested in the captive's stiff leg. Within the culture of the Mound Builders, certain persons born with physical deformities were greatly honored. Some of them actually became members of the ruling class, even though they may have been born of parents who were the lowest of common workers.

Cotauna spoke a few words to the guards who still ringed the battered young hunter. These men obeyed quickly, pulling O-Tah-Wah to his feet and marching him to the center of the temple's hard-packed clay floor. The light was better here. The handsome old priest now removed his antler headdress and knelt beside the trembling hunter. He did not touch the Lazy One, but he examined it from every angle. After some time, Cotauna still seemed quite interested in the new captive's strangely shaped limb. "I shall visit this man when he has learned our language," he told the others.

Clapping his hands sharply, Cotauna gave a brief command. The guards bowed quickly, then grabbed O-Tah-Wah by the arms and dragged him swiftly from the dimly lit temple into the brilliant light of day.

Two of the guards left them now, but the others hurried the blinking young captive out of the village. They walked through a grove of trees that shielded yet another strange structure. The small log building was nearly square, but it was otherwise much the same as the temple they had just left. A large heavy door in one side of the place was moved away from an opening leading into its dark interior. Roughly, the guards shoved O-Tah-Wah inside. Before he knew what had happened or realized that his captors had not followed him into the enclosure, the door had been pushed back into place. In the darkness, O-Tah-Wah heard them securing it. Slowly, a sickening knowledge soaked into his confused brain. The hunter's worst fears had come true—he was a prisoner of the Mound Builders!

It took several moments for the dazed and battered young captive to become accustomed to the darkness. When he could see better, O-Tah-Wah began limping around the walls of his prison, looking for a way out. There was none, and the heavy door was securely fastened on the outside. O-Tah-Wah felt miserable. He was hungry and thirsty as well as badly bruised from head to toe. The very gloom of the place was proof enough that escape was hopeless. The only light that entered came in through several small cracks around the door. There were also a few openings overhead, but these were far out of reach.

O-Tah-Wah sank sadly to the ground against one timbered wall. He leaned his head back in despair, thinking of his home and village and the free life of a hunter. Finally he slept.

Noises outside the little prison awakened the hunter several hours later. The door was being opened! O-Tah-Wah was just about to rush out into the light when five men were pushed and shoved through the door toward him. The opening was quickly resealed.

None of the five men saw O-Tah-Wah at first. He was still lying against the wall opposite the door, his legs sticking out into the room. One of the captives, a rather feeble-looking old man, stumbled over the Lazy One in the darkness. With a grunt of surprise, he stared down at O-Tah-Wah. He then began jabbering rapidly in a language that O-Tah-Wah could not understand. The words did not sound at all like those of the Mound Builders, however. O-Tah-Wah correctly guessed that these people were prisoners like himself.

They gathered around him, and he stood, dragging the Lazy One up with the rest of his body. One prisoner, much larger than the others, reminded O-Tah-Wah of a huge lumbering bear. O-Tah-Wah attempted to speak with him and was delighted to find that their languages were similar. Soon the others lost interest and curled up in various places to sleep. Before the giant lay down, however, he handed O-Tah-Wah a small leather pouch. In it the starving hunter found what he needed most—food! It was parched corn. Never had anything tasted so delicious. Even in his starved condition, however, O-Tah-Wah remembered the manners that his grandfather had taught him. Instead of eating all of the crunchy grain, O-Tah-Wah handed the little bag back to the giant after two handfuls. The big slave smiled a little at this politeness and from somewhere in the shadows produced a gourd half filled with water. O-Tah-Wah took it eagerly. This time he ignored etiquette completely and quickly drank every drop. The giant did not seem angry at all, and he simply took the empty gourd back to its place. He then lay down, turned his back on the new slave, and fell instantly asleep.

Much refreshed with even these tiny rations, O-Tah-Wah soon slept, too. Very soon would come the morning, and with it the beginning of an entirely new life for this hot-tempered young hunter from the north.

CHAPTER 3

Bruin

O-Tah-Wah was the first to waken. He had not slept much during the night due to hunger and the pains from his bumps and bruises. He had also been cold. How he missed the warmth of his buckskin robe! "Probably," he thought grimly, "some Mound Builder is even now sleeping soundly beneath my robe." The thought of such a thing made O-Tah-Wah angry once more. The anger gave him strength and warmed his cold and aching muscles. "If ever I can escape from this place," he told himself furiously, "I will take my revenge upon these 'Flatheads!'"

O-Tah-Wah's stumbling movements around the still-dark enclosure soon wakened the other captives. This was just as well, for within a few moments, the doorway was opened. O-Tah-Wah noticed that the other prisoners hurried out into the chilly dawn as if expecting something. He followed cautiously, knowing that there would be no chance of escape now. Since it would have taken several men to move the heavy door, the Mound Builders would no doubt be nearby, watching his every move.

Compared to the dark prison, even the pale morning's light seemed painfully bright. Blinking and squinting, O-Tah-Wah watched his companions. They were hurrying toward a skin tent some distance away. The little hut sat near the edge of the grove they had passed through the afternoon before. No one seemed to pay much attention to him, although several Mound Builders were standing about. Each one carried a bow and a full quiver of arrows, as well as a long, beautifully fashioned spear. And each one was magnificently dressed in skins decorated with beads, shellwork, and feathers. O-Tah-Wah could not help admiring these warriors. They carried themselves with great dignity and pride. They did not seem to think they were superior but to know it.

At the tent, the crippled hunter found the reason for all the haste his companions had shown. A fat old squaw was ladling out some sort of food with a gourd dipper. The stuff was slimy and dirty looking, but its aroma made O-Tah-Wah's mouth run with hunger. The others, he now discovered, had brought small wooden bowls to hold the corn gruel the old squaw had brewed for them. O-Tah-Wah had no bowl, but he approached the woman warily. Cupping both his hands together, he held them out toward the earthenware pot that was sitting in the edge of the fire. The squaw looked at O-Tah-Wah for some time, staring an especially long moment at the Lazy One. Then, with a wheezing chuckle, she dipped up a gob of the steaming goo and plopped it into the young man's waiting hands. O-Tah-Wah wanted to cry out in pain as the hot mush burned his fingers and palms, but he did not. For some reason, he wished to show no further fear or pain to these haughty people who had captured him.

The hunter hurried to a clean, grassy place and poured the hot food out on the ground. Wiping both stinging hands on his leggings, he then sat down and dipped the slimy stuff up with one finger. He ate every last drop. O-Tah-Wah would need to eat in order to regain his strength. From this moment on, he had but one objective in mind—escape!

Escape, however, was not to be so easy. The Mound Builders were a well-organized society. Unlike the rules of O-Tah-Wah's little village, the rules here were set. In the days and weeks to come, the young hunter was to learn much about these people and their way of life. Many other captives had been enslaved here. They had made plans for escape, too. But very few of them ever made their way to freedom. O-Tah-Wah would soon find out why.

He felt better now. The warm corn mush made a nice feeling under his belt. The headache was almost gone, too. There was to be no time to enjoy these comforts, however. Two Mound Builder guards moved up to him and by using signs and gestures, prodded him to join a small group of silent workers. O-Tah-Wah knew several of these sad-looking men to be the ones with whom he had spent the night. Two of the men glanced at him briefly, recognition showing for a moment in their eyes. Then they looked away, seeming not to care about him. It was clear to O-Tah-Wah that these men would be of little help in any escape plan. They had been prisoners too long. They no longer had the desire to think, much less to plan; they were slaves in every sense of the word. Even their minds were subject to the demands of the Mound Builders. Only the giant slave appeared to show any spark of life.

O-Tah-Wah shuddered inwardly as he watched the listless step and actions of his comrades as they were herded through the village and into the forest.

Once under the giant pines and the hemlock, the crippled hunter could not help feeling better. This was the kind of place he knew. The smells were familiar, the air was sweet, and the morning sun, falling in bright, ragged splotches here and there on the forest floor, warmed his neck and shoulders. He limped along almost happily, increasing his pace a little as his muscles continued to stretch and relax. The two guards noticed this, and one of them moved up quickly, gripping a short club in one muscular hand. O-Tah-Wah was in no mood for another beating. He fell obediently into line behind the other plodding workers. As he did so, he noticed the slight sneering smile that flickered across the face of the guard. It was plain that the guards no longer feared the hunter with the stiff leg. They were quite confident that he would make no further attempt at escape. O-Tah-Wah was glad to have them feeling this way; it would make his plans that much easier.

Finally, the band of men left the comfort of the big trees. In a grassy meadow at the forest's edge, O-Tah-Wah first saw the object that would take up nearly all of his waking hours in the coming days—a great burial mound. The mound was not even half finished. The raw, reddish earth and gravel of which it was being built was lumpy and uneven. There were high places and low places, with sunken areas showing on the sides as well as on the uncompleted top. Many people were already at work on the huge structure, which O-Tah-Wah guessed was somewhere between 500 and 600 paces around at the base. It was obvious that most of the men laboring here were of the Mound Builder race and not slaves at all. O-Tah-Wah was surprised at this; his grandfather's stories had led him to believe that the impressive earthworks of the Mound Builders were built by slave labor only.

O-Tah-Wah was not given much time to ponder the mysteries of building a burial mound. One of the guards gave him a woven basket with a leather carrying strap and pushed him roughly after the others. The rest of the work crew had already begun to fill their baskets with earth and loose gravel. The material was taken from the banks of a small stream that ran near the north side of the mound. Sometimes, the workers used sticks or flat stones for loosening the soil, but they usually found it simpler to scrape and scrabble away at the bank with their hands and fingers.

O-Tah-Wah went to work obediently, following the example of those near him. The basket he had been given was a marvel of skilled craftsmanship. O-Tah-Wah was puzzled that an object of such beauty would be used for this lowly task. He had much to learn about the level of skill and knowledge to which the Mound Builders had progressed.

The basket of earth was heavier than O-Tah-Wah had expected. Awkwardly, the hunter began to stagger up the steep, slippery wall of the mound, his load balanced carefully in the crook of one arm. The Lazy One was living up to its name on this cold, damp morning. For O-Tah-Wah, who was unaccustomed to such toil, the work was torture of the worst sort. The stiff leg finally gave out on O-Tah-Wah's fourth trip up the mound, and the hunter fell, spilling his load. What was worse, however, was that he slid nearly halfway down the side of the loosely compacted mound, his plunging body causing a small avalanche of pebbles and earth. The two Mound Builder guards were furious. With shouts and blows, they leaped upon him. Even before O-Tah-Wah had actually reached the bottom of the mound, the guards were beating him. Angrily, they jabbered away at the new slave, pointing and kicking at the pile of earth his body had brought down the slope.

O-Tah-Wah felt the signals coming on; his temper was rising. Desperately, the captive fought to swallow his fury, but each harsh word and every blow from fist and club fed the fires that were beginning to rage through his body. In another moment O-Tah-Wah would give into this rage and attack! Already the familiar red film was swimming before his eyes. Then a most marvelous and astonishing thing happened. A man's form, seeming to appear from nowhere, was suddenly between O-Tah-Wah and the two guards. The massive shoulders and the thick, muscular neck could belong to only one person: the giant, bear-like slave whom O-Tah-Wah had named "Bruin."

O-Tah-Wah's fury faded rapidly as in wonder, he watched Bruin take his part, keeping his powerful body between O-Tah-Wah and the shouting guards. Bruin answered the guards at times with a curious thick-tongued speech that seemed to come with great difficulty from his lips. At one point, he swung his huge, shaggy head around and pointed angrily at the Lazy One. O-Tah-Wah knew that Bruin was telling the guards that the crippled slave was unable to stand on the uneven footing of the mound. Never had anyone helped O-Tah-Wah in this way before. Bruin was doing this at great risk to himself, too! O-Tah-Wah hardly knew how to react to this kindness. He owed the big slave a great deal. Had O-Tah-Wah's temper given way again, it was quite likely that this time the guards would have killed him.

Several more Mound Builders, both guards and workers, had joined the argument by this time. Feeling braver with several more men backing them up, the first two guards began beating Bruin with their clubs. He did not fight back but lumbered off to his own work, having barely felt the blows that were rained on him.

The guards now put O-Tah-Wah to work loosening the gravel in the creek-side pit. No longer was he required to climb the shifting slope of the mound's side. Bruin had achieved his purpose. For the first time, O-Tah-Wah's thought about escape began to include one additional slave. After Bruin's kindness, how could O-Tah-Wah leave without him?

The early evening was falling when the guards finally allowed the slaves to stop working for the day. The Mound Builders who had been helping on the structure had drifted away earlier. When the small group of slaves shuffled wearily toward the stream, the ugly pile of earth, rock, and rubble was silent and deserted. O-Tah-Wah looked up at the mound several times as he scrubbed his body with the cold water. He could see no progress at all. In fact, the mound actually appeared smaller than it had when they had begun work that morning. O-Tah-Wah's lips pressed together in a tight, hard line. He could easily see that this work could go on for months, even years. His tired brain seemed to repeat a single word over and over again: *Escape! Escape! Escape!*

The walk back to the prison was a quiet one. Even though the guards had not carried so much as one basket of earth, they seemed as tired and listless as the slaves they watched. O-Tah-Wah noticed with some excitement that they paid little attention to the prisoners at all. Their weapons were slung carelessly over their shoulders. Their eyes seemed intent only on picking the easiest walking places through the open glades surrounding the village. For a wild, heart-pounding moment, O-Tah-Wah had an impulse to simply dart away into the trees and keep on running. Everything in his better judgment told him this was insane, however, and he fought down the impulse. His grandfather had often spoken of the near impossibility of escaping from the Flatheads, and he had been right so far. Surely, the Mound Builders had very good ways of preventing attempts at escape. O-Tah-Wah wisely decided to continue his work for a few more days until he had time to study the chances of escape. He knew, however, that he dare not wait until the trees had lost their leaves. Once the ground was covered with snow, the Mound Builders would be able to track him down with no trouble at all. As the guards fastened the jail door behind him, O-Tah-Wah made his decision—the escape must come before the next full moon.

Feeling weary, but with hope in his heart, O-Tah-Wah burrowed into the foul-smelling husks that covered the jail's earthen floor. Soon, he fell into exhausted sleep. Toward morning, the captive had a marvelous dream. He was free again! The trees spoke to him in their own language. The secrets of the heavens were explained by the birds, and the small creatures of the forest called him by name. The most wonderful part of all, however, was that in the dream, he was no longer alone—he had a friend!

The dawn came slowly on this third morning of his captivity. O-Tah-Wah was surprised by the fact that the guards had not yet dragged him off to the day's work. He sat up, the dream still fresh and clear in his mind. The other slaves were stirring, too, but for the first time since he had known them, they were smiling. Bruin tapped O-Tah-Wah's shoulder and then pointed to one of the cracks between the great timbers that made up the stout walls of their little prison. O-Tah-Wah shifted the Lazy One awkwardly until he was able to put one eye to the crack. Outside, the grayish light of morning was almost blotted out by low-lying clouds and a steady, driving rain. One of the slaves then imitated the work of digging while shaking his head "no". O-Tah-Wah quickly read the sign language to mean there would be no work today.

The Mound Builder chieftain in charge of construction on the burial mound had wisely decided to call off the day's work. The rain would loosen the earth and gravel to the point where the workers might dislodge large portions of the carefully built banks. This would make more work than before.

O-Tah-Wah, seated in a fairly dry corner of the stockade, did not care why the work had been stopped. He was only grateful that it had been, whatever the reason. He had just fallen asleep again when he was awakened by the sound of the door being moved aside. The other slaves got up quickly and hurried out into the rain. O-Tah-Wah could not understand. Two guards were at the doorway, but they did not seem to care if the captives came out or not. O-Tah-Wah moved cautiously to the doorway, trying to decide what would be the wise thing to do. Peering through the rain, he caught sight of the great bulk of his friend Bruin. The crippled hunter was shocked at what he saw.

Bruin, the giant who had dared to come between a slave and the guards, was begging! O-Tah-Wah watched as the big slave stood humbly, head hanging, before the doorway of one of the round dwelling units. The rain had soaked his ragged skin clothing, and his long black hair lay wet and gleaming upon his face and neck. He appeared to be saying nothing at all but just standing there in the rain, his head sadly bowed. In one great fist, he held his crude little wooden bowl. He did not hold the bowl forward but merely left it at his side, ready in case someone might throw him some small bit of food or a bone that had not been picked clean. It was a sight that might make a grown man cry or feel the depths of pity. This was not how O-Tah-Wah felt, however.

O-Tah-Wah was furious. He limped out into the clearing, paying no attention to the shock of the cold rain as it splashed across his bare shoulders. The Lazy One began to ache as he hurried toward the big slave, who still stood unmoving before the door. Angrily, he snatched at Bruin's bowl, knocking it into the mud as he did so. The big slave turned toward him, a puzzled look on his homely face. O-Tah-Wah's temper was up again. He could not stand to see such a great, strong man begging for food from his captors. Fiercely, O-Tah-Wah pushed at Bruin's side, knocking him a few steps backward, toward the stockade. Bruin's eyes narrowed slightly at O-Tah-Wah's surprising behavior. When O-Tah-Wah pushed the giant again, Bruin struck back with one huge, clenched fist. The knuckles caught O-Tah-Wah right on the ear. He was knocked to his knees in the mud, his head ringing from the force of Bruin's almost casual blow.

O-Tah-Wah stayed down, knowing that Bruin would undoubtedly knock him down again if he arose. It was surprising how rapidly his temper cooled as he squatted there in the cold mud. He peered up at Bruin. From this angle, the giant looked like a mountain of flesh. Slowly, O-Tah-Wah began to realize how much food was needed to keep this great frame from hunger. Reaching behind him, O-Tah-Wah located the little bowl and held it up to Bruin. Taking the wooden object with his left hand, the giant pulled O-Tah-Wah to his feet. Bruin did not smile, but neither did he look angry. He walked back to the door of the dwelling and stood in the same position he had before. His huge body needed food, and he knew of no other way to get any.

O-Tah-Wah glanced toward the guards. They had not moved from their sheltered spot beside the slave quarters. Although they had watched the scuffle, they apparently had not found it of any interest. The crippled hunter was not sure now just what he could and could not do. He decided to try moving off through the village to see if the guards would object. Calmly, O-Tah-Wah turned his back on the Mound Builders and started walking toward the circular log houses that clustered near the priest's mound. One of the guards followed the hunter at a distance but made no attempt to stop him.

O-Tah-Wah limped along in the mud and rain, determined to take this chance to scout the Mound Builders' village. Some of the things he was to see would show him how difficult his escape would be.

He had not gone completely through the village when he was surprised to see two warriors walking toward him. "You will come with us," they ordered. Hardly waiting to see if O-Tah-Wah was following, they turned and led the way to the temple.

Through the curtain of falling rain, O-Tah-Wah saw the temple. It sat on its own man-made hill, looking frightening and severe. Shyly, O-Tah-Wah entered the building. The two warriors who had brought him stopped just inside the entranceway, but O-Tah-Wah moved on toward the fire. The steady blaze lighted both the great hall and the man who sat there waiting for the slave he had summoned. It was Cotauna.

O-Tah-Wah recognized the priest immediately, for the old man was not wearing the wolf-mask this time. "Do you understand our language now?" Cotauna asked. His voice was kindly and soft. The crippled slave noted with surprise that the leader did not look well. Cotauna was thin and tired looking, and his eyes seemed dull and without hope.

"Yes," O-Tah-Wah answered. "I can understand many of your words, but sometimes I do not understand the Mound Builders hearts."

Cotauna nodded somewhat sadly. "The way you feel is not surprising, since we keep you here against your wishes. But do you not see how much better we live than do those of the smaller tribes such as yours?"

"No!" O-Tah-Wah almost spat the word in the old man's face. "There is *no* better way than the way of freedom." O-Tah-Wah was becoming angry. "Why are you asking me these things?" he demanded bluntly.

"I would learn about the ways of other people," Cotauna replied. "Soon it will be time for me to die. I find myself wondering about many things now. Not only am I concerned about the afterlife, but also I worry about my people. Sometimes it seems that we are moving in wrong directions. You have a crippled leg. We believe that sometimes such things are a sign of great wisdom, for your body has been touched by a spirit. Therefore, I wish to hear your thoughts."

"Then you shall hear them!" snapped O-Tah-Wah. "My village is poor, and we lack the great wisdom and wealth of the Mound Builders. But there are two important ways in which we rise above you: never would we hold another man, even an enemy, in bondage; and as for peace and happiness in the next life, we trust the Great Spirit."

Cotauna sat frowning and thinking in complete silence for a long, long time. O-Tah-Wah, whose eyes never left the priest, began to suspect that Cotauna had forgotten he was even there. Then, at last, the old man raised one skinny hand and made a slight motion. Instantly, the two warriors hurried O-Tah-Wah out of the room. The visit was over.

News of the meeting between Cotauna and O-Tah-Wah spread swiftly throughout the village, but no one knew what had taken place. O-Tah-Wah told them nothing.

CHAPTER 4

A Secret Discovered

The snow came sweeping down out of a heavy, gray-speckled sky. A west wind moaned through the pines as it covered the village with rapidly drifting snow.

O-Tah-Wah sat up slowly, trying to stop the constant shivering and shaking of his body. Bruin was awake, too, feeding the fire with a slightly green log. The giant then began to bank the flames with ashes in order to keep the fire from burning itself out too quickly. He spoke a few words to O-Tah-Wah, then curled up in his skin robes so close to the heat that he was in real danger of being burned.

The Lazy One was aching severely this morning, but O-Tah-Wah was too happy to notice. For the first time in longer than he could remember, he did not feel the burning heat within his body. Many weeks he had lain in the stockade, sick and hardly conscious. Bruin had cared for him whenever he could, bringing bits of food that were dropped into bowls of hot water. Most of the time, however, O-Tah-Wah had merely shivered under the foul-smelling skins that the slaves had been given. O-Tah-Wah had lost all track of time. He could not get outside to look at the moon or even catch a glimpse of the winter sun in order to judge the season by its angle.

But this morning was different. O-Tah-Wah knew that now he was getting well. The fever was finally gone, and though weak, he felt almost like himself again. Bruin could tell this, too. And as he peeked out from the mound of skins, his ugly brutal face broke into a smile that to O-Tah-Wah was almost beautiful.

O-Tah-Wah could not remember how long he had been sick. He guessed that it was now nearly mid-winter. The entire season of autumn was lost to him. Work on the mound had stopped long ago when the ground had frozen too hard for digging. The crippled slave had been left to die in the stockade while the more able workers were taken into the homes and temples to do chores that were needed in winter. Because Bruin was too big and clumsy for this work, he was left in the stockade with O-Tah-Wah.

The log prison was hardly guarded at all now. There was no need for it. Anyone trying to escape could easily be tracked through the snow. Also, a runaway slave would have to eat, and in this weather, game would be very hard to find. The most important reason no one ran away at this time of year, however, was the lack of warm skins for clothing and foot coverings.

O-Tah-Wah knew that there would be no chance for escape until the spring. But preparations must begin now. As his strength returned, he would begin to plan. And when the time of floods was at hand, he would go. Bruin would be asked, too.

The giant suddenly started speaking, his voice barely penetrating the rumpled mound of skins he had piled over himself. "When are you planning your escape from the Flatheads?" he asked bluntly. As O-Tah-Wah jumped up in surprise, the voice continued. "Yes, my little friend, I was watching you before you became sick. I know what you were thinking about. Had you not become ill, I am sure that you would have made your attempt long ago. Now you must wait until the snow has gone." Bruin laughed loudly as he finished speaking. Peering out from under a worn moose-hide robe, he had seen such a look of idiotic surprise on O-Tah-Wah's face that he could not stop laughing. His bellows shook the log walls that surrounded them. O-Tah-Wah finally laughed, too, although he was more shocked than amused.

"How did you find this out?" he asked when the laughter had finally died away.

"You were not very clever," Bruin replied. He sat up and pulled the thin, ragged coverings closer over his legs. Hunching his broad, powerful shoulders, he squatted near the smoldering fire and gazed intently at his friend. "I think that some of the other slaves may suspect it, as well," he continued. "I watched you as you walked in the village. Your eyes missed nothing. The dog pen seemed to be your favorite place. Why did you spend so much time near those wild, foul-smelling beasts?"

O-Tah-Wah could think of no reason for trying to keep his "secret" any longer. It was plain that Bruin knew what he was planning. Feeling very foolish, O-Tah-Wah decided that he might as well begin. He vowed silently, however, that Bruin would be the only one he would ask to come along. Hunching closer to the heat, O-Tah-Wah sat quietly for many minutes thinking back over the months of his captivity.

"Wake up!" Bruin growled after a time. "I asked you why you were always trying to get near the dog pens."

"I am sorry," O-Tah-Wah answered quickly. "My mind was running like the deer. Yes, good friend, I *am* going to escape. You are right, too, that I would have made my attempt long

ago, had the sickness not taken me. When the spring comes, however, I will go. You must come, too, but the others should not be told. More than two traveling together would be too easy to track."

"The dogs," Bruin reminded him. "What about the dogs?"

O-Tah-Wah shook his head at his own stupidity and continued quickly. "I was trying to make friends with them, or at least let them get to know my scent a little. I was sure that the Flatheads would use the dogs to track a runaway slave. Of course, we would head for the nearest river, but I do not know for certain where this would be. We might have to travel several days' journey before finding a stream in which to travel north. Every time I passed the dog pens and every time the guards allowed us free time for begging, I tried to drop in a bit of food or a bone. Perhaps the dogs know me a little now."

"You are a fool!" Bruin growled. He swung his huge body around and stood up. After he had rearranged the ragged skins around his shoulders, he continued. "I have been a slave here for nine summers. What you do not know is that this village, fine and grand as it may seem to people like us, is but a small outpost. It is only one of many, many great villages that spread out from this area southward, eastward, and even to the west. A good hunter could travel many days in any of these directions before he would pass beyond the land of the Mound Builders!" Bruin sat down again, arranging the skins like a small tent around his body. O-Tah-Wah smiled quietly to himself. Bruin, he knew, had been a slave too long. His friend's mind must be slipping. Surely there could be no greater village anywhere than the one in which they now found themselves. He dared not challenge the big slave's truthfulness, however. "What you say may be true," he grunted, "but what does this have to do with my attempt at making friends with the tracking dogs?"

"Because there are many dogs in many villages!" Bruin snapped. "Some of these are trained not only to track, but also to attack and kill any runaway they are following. The moment a slave is found missing, special runners are sent out to all nearby villages. Many, many men and dogs then join in the chase. It is great sport for them, and very few, indeed, are those who manage to escape. The search may go on from one full moon to the next. Sometimes, there will be more men on the chase than live in this entire village! Yes, my stiff-legged, hot-tempered brother, trying to make friends with the dogs of our village is hardly worth the chance you are taking. You must stop this at once!"

O-Tah-Wah stared intently across the fire, looking into the face of his friend. Somehow, the big man's voice held the ring of truth. O-Tah-Wah found himself beginning to believe these incredible stories. "What if these things are true, or even partly true?" he asked himself with growing alarm. "It is little wonder, then, that slaves taken by the Mound Builders never return!"

Bruin had been watching his small companion intently. He read quite clearly the unspoken thoughts that were passing through O-Tah-Wah's mind. The giant felt sorry for him. Had he not become ill, O-Tah-Wah would have learned all of these things for himself. For the past three moons, however, he had been lying in the stockade, nearer to death than life. Bruin took no credit for the fact that, had it not been for him, O-Tah-Wah would never have recovered at all, much less be talking of escape.

"Little brother," Bruin began after a long silence, "there is something else you should be told about the Flatheads. Do you remember the priest who wears the horns of a deer? He is the one who came to look at your 'Lazy One' just after you were captured."

"Yes, I remember him well," O-Tah-Wah replied. A smile crossed his face as he recalled his terror when he first saw this important man.

"Well," continued Bruin, "he is a very old and important man, and the whisperings in the village have it that he has been very sick for almost a full moon. Do you know what this means?"

"No." O-Tah-Wah's reply was somewhat sharp. He wondered why Bruin was changing the subject. This was a good time for them to plan their escape. No guards were nearby, and the other slaves were all off in the village. He did not care about the health of the Flathead priest anyway!

Bruin reached across the fire and placed his rough, huge hand on O-Tah-Wah's shoulder. "If he should die," he whispered, "some of the slaves will die, too!" He did not release his grip as he finished speaking, but continued to hold onto O-Tah-Wah's shoulder, as if to emphasize his point.

O-Tah-Wah, shocked and frightened, frowned at the big man. "But why is this true?" he asked quickly.

"If he dies," Bruin began, his voice again dropping almost to a whisper, "he will be buried in a new mound like the one we are now finishing. Slaves will then be executed in order that their spirits might serve and protect the priest's spirit in the Next World!"

"But what is there to protect?" O-Tah-Wah asked. His mind was struggling to understand what these words meant in terms of his escape in the spring.

"When Cotauna dies," Bruin answered, "a great deal of wealth will die with him. His many strands of pearls will be broken and scattered in the grave. The finest flint spears and the most beautiful chest plates of banded slate will be 'killed' by breaking, and they also will go into the tomb. The spirits of these items can then be used by the spirit of Cotauna. Pipes of pipestone will be included, as well as the great ceremonial spears made of shiny, black Spirit Stone! This stone is brought at great cost and peril from the Mountains-of-Summer-Snow. I have heard other slaves say that it is a westward journey of 200 days to this place!"

Both men were whispering now, for if one of the guards should happen to come near, it would be very dangerous to be caught discussing such a subject. Bruin, seeing that O-Tah-Wah believed him, went on with the story.

"If the high priest Cotauna should die," Bruin whispered earnestly, "you must try to escape just as soon as the news reaches you." He did not go on, for they both knew that should the old priest become more ill than he now was, the guards might be doubled. O-Tah-Wah and Bruin would not be the only slaves desperate for freedom. Unlike O-Tah-Wah, the others had already seen what happened when an important man died.

Bruin suddenly began laughing softly to himself. O-Tah-Wah was shocked by this behavior, for he could see nothing amusing about the problems that faced them. "Why do you laugh?" he snarled, the old problem of temper moving forward again. "Is it because you find the prospect of death so pleasant?"

"Ah!" Bruin said, still smiling a little. "I can see that my little wolverine is getting well. Once again he becomes angry too quickly, even before he knows the cause. Calm down, forget your hurt, and I shall tell you a story. It is the tale of a very wise man who, captured and threatened with torture, found his own method of escape."

O-Tah-Wah was immediately interested. Anything that had to do with escape was of the utmost importance to him now. Eagerly, he scooted his skinny body nearer the fire. Trying to arrange the ragged, moldy skins around his shivering shoulders, he studied the man on the other side of the low flames. Light from the smoky fire threw strange and changing highlights across the many planes of the giant's dark, broad face. Deep shadows cast by his nose and chin made the features appear even uglier than usual. His eyes, small and deeply set under bony brows, seemed to disappear altogether as he sat up straighter and prepared to begin.

Outside, the wind was rising, piling billows of snow high along the sides of the stockade. Far from being unwelcome, the snow was a blessing, for as it packed itself against the log walls, it helped to hold the meager heat inside. Thus the cold snow actually made the slaves' quarters warmer. Howling winds driving in from the great, open plains of the Southwest bumped and rattled the logs of their little prison. But O-Tah-Wah paid no attention. He was waiting for Bruin to speak.

CHAPTER 5

Bruin's Story

"We slaves did not know the name of the trader from the south, but his courage and kindness made him a friend to all. After several visits, we noticed that he always wore an ornament in his hair. It was most cleverly fashioned, and when one of the Flatheads asked him about it, he showed the object to all of us. It was a comb made by cutting thin slits through half the length of a small brightly colored turtle shell. 'Turtle Shell' seemed a good name, so this was what we called him.

Turtle Shell was not a slave, at least not at first. The slaves who knew his funny-sounding language said that he came from a land far to the south. In this strange place, they said, winter never came and snow never fell. Of course, I did not believe this, but the trader did have some items to sell that were unlike anything I had ever seen here.

Each year, in the time of melting snow, Turtle Shell would come into our village. He must have been a minor chief, for always with him were 20 warriors. Turtle Shell himself carried no weapons. He needed none, for his braves never left him alone. This protection was wise, for Turtle Shell brought great wealth: beads of shell, feathers of glowing color, necklaces, and many other beautiful things. Among his most highly prized items were the teeth of a great animal. Turtle Shell said it lived in the waters of the hot swamplands near his home. This beast, he claimed, had many, many teeth, and jaws that opened large enough to swallow a child in one gulp! I would not have believed this story except that the teeth were huge and seemed to be real.

For several years, Turtle Shell came to this village. At first, he was welcomed here. The chiefs and priests were glad to trade with him. All he wanted in return was flint, freshwater pearls, or copper. Since all of these things were fairly easy to get, the Mound Builders were eager to make exchanges. Each year, however, Turtle Shell became more and more popular with the people. When not busy with his trading, he would talk to those who could understand his language. They would then pass his sayings along to others, until the whole village knew of his clever ideas. Some of the things he told us were very strange, but many times there was great wisdom in his words. Jealous, the priests and chiefs of the Mound Builders began to look upon Turtle Shell with narrow eyes.

One thing made the priests especially angry. As Turtle Shell talked with the villagers, he made fun of the Mound Builder practice of burying weapons and jewelry with their dead. This, the trader pointed out, was a terrible waste. When a person of wealth died in Turtle Shell's village, the man's possessions were given to his oldest son. In this way, families kept their fine things from generation to generation. Nothing was wasted. Turtle Shell went on to say that since, after death, a man entered the Spirit World, weapons and tools would be of little use to him anyway. When the priests heard what the trader was telling the villagers, they set out to confront Turtle Shell with their grievances.

The trader was talking to a group of slaves when the little party of chiefs and priests arrived at his camp. When they told him of their anger at the ideas he was spreading in the village, he simply laughed at them. This was most certainly a foolish thing to do. Little Eyes, a minor chieftain who was very jealous of Turtle Shell, leaped forward and slapped the trader across the face. Turtle Shell's braves, lounging nearby, leaped up. In a few seconds, a battle was going on. The small band fought bravely and well, but the great numbers of Mound Builders who entered the fray soon overpowered them. Four of Turtle Shell's braves were killed, several wounded, and the rest taken captive. Turtle Shell was imprisoned with them.

With their 'enemies' now in the stockade, the priests wasted no time in spreading lies and rumors about Turtle Shell and his warriors. The people of the village believed these stories, and soon most of the tribe was in a fury for Turtle Shell's blood! Little Eyes could not have been more pleased. The hated trader would no longer be spreading discontent among the people.

Only a few days had gone by before Little Eyes began talking with the priests about the necessity of Turtle Shell's death. He argued and insisted, bullying the priests into listening to him. 'This stranger,' he said over and over again, 'deserves to be put to death. Did he not ridicule our ancient customs? Also, he has been seen more than once encouraging the slaves to overthrow their masters. He must be made an example, lest other tribes send such persons into our camps to trouble us!'

Although the priests and rulers generally disliked Turtle Shell, they liked the exotic trade items he brought into their village each spring. They had to admit, however, that the words of Little Eyes made sense. Reluctantly, they let themselves believe that the jealous young chieftain was right, and they agreed to put Turtle Shell to death. By this time, two more of his braves had died of wounds received in the brief battle. It was decided that Turtle Shell's remaining braves would be left alive but forced to do slave labor for the rest of their days.

This terrible news was not long in reaching Turtle Shell and his braves. Also, it was now known that Little Eyes would be in charge of the execution.

Turtle Shell did not sleep at all the night he learned of his fate. Lying awake and troubled, he thought of many things. He knew Little Eyes well. There could be no doubt that a terrible, lingering death by torture awaited him. Little Eyes would not miss this opportunity to take his revenge, while at the same time being the center of attention for the entire village. The trader also felt sure that his torture would be done publicly, so that all might see his shame. He was not afraid of death, but he wished to die with dignity. He thought hard and long.

Toward morning a breeze sprang up. Its soft sighing reminded Turtle Shell of the whispering waves near his own village far away on the Great Salt Sea. The sound seemed to help him think, too, for at last he had an idea. It did not come to him a moment too soon, for dawn was breaking.

The trader felt sure that he would have a few days to put his plan into action. Little Eyes would want the sport to last as long as possible. Therefore Turtle Shell was not surprised when, shortly after dawn, he was dragged out of the stockade. Very soon, he found himself lashed securely to a thick post in a cleared area near the center of the village. He began his little act immediately.

As the villagers came by to laugh and taunt the trader, he asked each one to bring some items that he needed. It was with great surprise that they heard his strange requests. Everyone who passed was asked for the same four items: bear grease, dog hair, blue clay, and willow leaves. The Flatheads shook their heads in wonder and of course no one brought him anything. While many of the people secretly liked the young man from the south, no one intended to anger the priests by aiding the prisoner in any way. When the villagers failed to honor his requests, Turtle Shell did not become angry or sad but laughed and joked with the Mound Builders as though he had no cares at all.

The sun had not reached the top of the sky before the priests and chiefs heard of the prisoner's odd behavior. All of the people were curious. What did he want to do with these four common things for which he continually asked? Why was he so cheerful when he was facing days of torture and a lingering death? All sorts of ideas were set forth, guesses were made, and opinions given, but no one knew the answer. Little work was done on this day, for by now all of the people were busy trying to solve the riddle.

No one was more interested than Little Eyes. How he hated this trader! Turtle Shell should be begging for mercy, trying to break his bonds, or crying in despair. Instead, he had all the village talking about him, and he seemed as cheerful as ever. Little Eyes decided to see for himself. He strode towards the prisoner, walking with exaggerated dignity and style.

Turtle Shell was pleased to see his enemy approaching. So far the plan was working! He spread his face into a wide, happy smile and waited for the jealous chief to begin.

'I understand there are some things you would like to have,' Little Eyes snarled, his face twisted into a cruel sneer. People were gathering quickly now, sensing that something was about to happen. Little Eyes folded his arms and stared haughtily at the man tied to the post.

'Yes, it is true,' Turtle Shell replied easily. Then he raised his voice slightly, for he wished to be sure all could hear. 'I have been told that you, O great chief, are the only one who has learned why I have asked for these four things. You and you alone are not without wisdom among the Mound Builders!' The onlookers murmured in surprise and turned admiring glances upon Little Eyes. Until now, most of them had thought of him as rather stupid. If he had solved this difficult riddle so easily, however, he must be clever indeed.

Little Eyes' mouth fell open in shock. For a moment, he was completely confused. When he looked around at all of the villagers, however, he quickly caught himself and for their benefit managed to look very wise. The people continued to watch their chief. It was obvious that they expected him to tell them the answer to the riddle. Although he had not the faintest notion of what the answer was, he did not want the others to know this. A few moments passed and finally he turned around and walked slowly away toward his dwelling place.

Once the door was in place behind him, Little Eyes threw his feather mantle to the floor in a rage. The hated trader had tricked him yet again, but the worst part of it was that he was not even sure how he had been fooled! Little Eyes was furious!

All day long, Turtle Shell continued to laugh and talk with the villagers. As each villager passed by, Turtle Shell asked for the bear grease, dog hair, blue clay, and willow leaves. While these items could have been found in a few moments by the smallest child, no one brought them to him. The trader was not disappointed, for he had expected this would happen.

Early the next morning, even before dawn, Little Eyes appeared before the captive. His anger was terrible, and he began at once to describe the methods of torture he would use. The trader knew that there could be no escape for him. All he desired now was a quick and merciful death without the indignity and disgrace of public torture. His plan was working well.

When Little Eyes finished telling his prisoner of the means by which he would be tormented and mutilated during the coming days, Turtle Shell asked a question. 'Tell me,' he began, 'how it is that you learned my secret so easily. Others have tried to guess why I need the clay, the leaves, the grease, and the dog hair. But you know about the magic paste of my people. How did you learn this?'

'I know many things,' Little Eyes boasted. His eyes were mere slits in his handsome face as he tried hard to out-think the trader. 'Yes, I know all about this magic paste of which you speak,' he lied. The chief felt smug, confident that he was winning this battle of wits. Little did he realize how cleverly Turtle Shell was leading him into a trap.

'Then,' continued the trader, 'you must know also that a warrior who is wearing this paste cannot be killed, providing the potion is freshly made each morning.'

Little Eyes almost laughed aloud. How simple it was to outsmart this stupid trader from the south. The chief was very excited. If what Turtle Shell said was true, he must learn this magic. In a short time, he could become the greatest warrior his people had ever known. Now he must see the charm medicine made in order to learn exactly how it was done.

'As you say,' the chief began, 'I know all about the magic paste. However, it has been a long time since I have seen it prepared, and my memory fails me. Also, I do not believe that a dishonest and lying trader such as yourself really knows the correct way of preparing the materials. Therefore, I myself will bring you what you desire. Then I will watch. Do not doubt that I can easily tell whether you really are able to make this medicine as it should be made.' As he finished speaking, Little Eyes looked around carefully. He was satisfied that, due to the early hour, they were still quite alone. Then he hurried away to gather the four needed materials.

He soon returned with a basket. Under one arm, he held a clay jar that was made in the shape of a human head. The odor proved that the small brown vessel contained bear grease. Little Eyes worked quickly now, for he was afraid someone would come along and see what was happening. He cut Turtle Shell's hands and arms loose with a few strokes of his flint knife. Leaving the thongs that bound the prisoner at the waist and those that bound his legs and feet, the chief hurriedly pushed the 'magic' ingredients into the prisoner's hands.

Turtle Shell had trouble working at first, for his fingers were numb from the leather lashings. Nevertheless, he began combining the four items. When he had made a large gob of the sticky mess, he proudly held it out to the chief. 'With this smeared over my body, no arrow can harm me. But of course you know this already.'

Little Eyes was about to call the trader a liar, but at that moment several villagers arrived. They were soon asking questions about the magic potion. This gave Turtle Shell the chance to begin the final part of his plan. Before the chief could stop him, he shouted to the onlookers. 'Waken the village!' he roared. 'Very soon now you shall see the wisdom of Little Eyes, your chief.'

Most of the Flatheads were awake by now, so in a few moments nearly the entire village had gathered to see the excitement. Turtle Shell smiled his bravest smile and called out to some of the Mound Builders in a loud, friendly voice. When the people were packed closely around him, Turtle Shell began to apply the smelly mess to his upper body. As he did so, he told the people what he meant to do. 'Little Eyes is the only one of you who knows my secret,' he announced dramatically. Little Eyes threw out his chest a little as he noticed the admiring looks of the people.

'Bring up four of your finest bowmen,' Turtle Shell shouted. Before the chief had time to object, the trader had told the crowd what he intended to do. 'Select your sharpest arrow,' he told the four who were chosen, 'and stand here in front of me. I have covered my chest with the magic potion, and Little Eyes, your wise chief, knows that now no arrow can pierce my body!'

Little Eyes was confused and angry. Things were moving too rapidly for him. He could not understand how all of this had happened. It was plain that the crowd thought him a hero. Little Eyes enjoyed this admiration, but somehow he felt he was being tricked. But why would Turtle Shell propose such a test if the potion was not really magic?

'Now will the true wisdom of Little Eyes be shown,' Turtle Shell said quietly. He no longer needed to shout, for although many people were watching, no one uttered a sound. They stood in awe of this trader who could make such powerful medicine. 'Draw your bows!' Turtle Shell's voice continued clear and steady. He raised his chin and squared his shoulders against the post. 'Aim for my heart, and when I give the word, you will shoot.' There was not a sound in the entire crowd. Even their breathing had stopped.

'Fire!'

Four arrows plunged through Turtle Shell's chest and into the post behind him. Two of these passed through his heart, killing him instantly.

At first the crowd was too stunned to do anything except stare at the body of the trader, still standing and pinned against the post. After a few moments, however, Little Eyes noticed that some of the people were smiling. Then a low rumble of sound could be heard. In horror, the chief realized that they were laughing—laughing at *him*!

The arrogant chief was the last one to realize he had been made a fool. The young trader's plan had worked. His death had been quick and painless, and what was more important, he had died with dignity."

CHAPTER 6

Preparing for Escape

The days and weeks passed slowly now. Bruin and O-Tah-Wah had no work to do. The cold had stopped almost all of the outdoor activity in the village. O-Tah-Wah was growing stronger every day. His healing body was constantly hungry, and it was all Bruin could do to beg enough food to keep them both alive. The slaves were still given corn once a day by the Mound Builders, but it was never enough. O-Tah-Wah was very grateful to Bruin. He told himself that he must repay this gentle giant for saving his life, but he did not know how this could be done. The crippled slave could not know of the surprising way that he would one day settle his debt.

Winter was still upon them, but now there were times when the cold seemed less severe. Finally, during one of these bright, windless days, Bruin decided that the Lazy One should be given some exercise. "I think," he announced after he and O-Tah-Wah had finished a meal of fishheads, "that you are ready now to come with me into the village to beg. Also, there is something I wish you to see."

O-Tah-Wah could hardly see at all as they stumbled along behind their grumbling guard. The darkened prison was all he had known for so many weeks that the sun shimmering across the snow nearly struck him blind. He could not tell the direction they took, or even exactly where they were in the village.

At last they entered one of the large round houses. Once the door was closed, O-Tah-Wah could see a little. In all his weeks with the Mound Builders, this was the first time he had been able to enter one of the houses. It was the most fascinating thing he had ever seen.

The building was warm and comfortable. Its hard-packed earthen floor was now covered with several layers of animal skins. The skins made the footing soft, and they effectively kept out the cold. Near the center of the room was a rectangular framework of poles, covered with large squares of bark. Within this enclosure a fire burned brightly. The wooden heat shield kept the residents from being too warm as they sat on the raised benches near the fire.

The guard immediately sat down near the fire and began rubbing his cold legs and arms. O-Tah-Wah hung back, watching Bruin to see how he should act. Bruin was talking to a fat little man who was seated cross-legged on a low bench near one wall. The Flathead was working flint.

Both slaves moved closer to watch. O-Tah-Wah knew that Bruin sometimes helped the toolmaker. In fact, it was from him that Bruin had begged much of the food that had kept them both alive during the early winter.

After a few moments, Bruin began to work. His job was the most unskilled part but one in which his great strength was useful. Seating himself near the fire, the giant took a smooth hammerstone in his right hand and began to strike steadily at a block of pink-and-brown flint. The heavy, measured blows occasionally resulted in a sliver being chipped off. It was these splinters that the stoneworker would use. Each one could be fashioned into a useful object: a knife, a spearhead, a drill, a punch, or a scraper.

O-Tah-Wah could not pull his eyes away from the clever fingers of the stoneworker. Since he had first been taken captive, the crippled hunter had been fascinated by the skill of the Mound Builders. He was also aware of how far advanced their tools and weapons were when compared to those he had been taught to make. Now he was to be given the opportunity of seeing how they were made.

The toolmaker, who made most of the tools and weapons for the village, seemed to be most happy at his work. As Bruin's fragments fell from the flint core, the toolmaker examined each one carefully, turning it over and over in his pudgy fingers. Finding one that suited him, the fat little man picked up a small stone hammer. When the toolmaker used the instrument, it bounced and quivered with every blow. Using delicate, careful strokes, he tapped the flint along its edges, patiently working it into the shape he desired. Often he smiled at the others, and sometimes he moistened the stone with his tongue so he could better see the beauty of its color.

When the blade was correctly shaped, the toolmaker laid his hammer aside and finished the work with a small bone awl. The arrowhead he had made was strong, sharp, and beautiful. The man was a master worker of stone.

Bruin worked hard for almost the entire day. O-Tah-Wah helped wherever possible, but he spent most of his time watching the craftsman at work. O-Tah-Wah could see the advantage of one person making flint objects for the entire village. No wonder his own people had never learned to fashion tools of such quality! O-Tah-Wah knew that he must talk with the elders of his clan when he returned home. Perhaps they would listen to some new ways of doing things. He, O-Tah-Wah, would show them how.

Crack! Bruin's hammerstone struck the colorful flint core an especially sharp blow. At almost the same moment, a long flake of the smooth, brittle stone bounced off O-Tah-Wah's sleeve. No one seemed to notice the jagged stone fragment that lay on the skin floor near the Lazy One. O-Tah-Wah looked quickly around him. The guard was half hidden behind the fire box, but the toolmaker was busy grinding a smooth base on the finished arrow point. Now was the time! O-Tah-Wah pretended to have a great fit of coughing. Dropping to one knee, he continued to cough and gag until his body was almost bent double. Half turning, he shot one hand down and grabbed the four-inch sliver of stone. The hand crept under his ragged clothes as he straightened up. When nearly erect, O-Tah-Wah was suddenly terrified by a roar of rage. Bruin had seen the whole thing. Leaping across the benches, the giant grabbed O-Tah-Wah around the neck. As one huge hand held him, the other smashed into the side of his head. O-Tah-Wah was stunned almost senseless. He nearly fell, but Bruin yanked him to his feet once more. The flint scrap was torn angrily from his hand and thrown on the pile with the others. Then Bruin picked up O-Tah-Wah and kicked the door open with one foot. With a mighty heave, the huge man hurled him nearly six feet through the air. O-Tah-Wah landed in a deep snow bank where he lay, stunned and aching.

The guard was laughing mightily at the way the giant had taken care of the little thief. The toolmaker was laughing, too, but as he did so, he slapped Bruin on the shoulder to show his appreciation for the big man's loyalty.

Bruin left the warm, bark house angrily. He yanked O-Tah-

Wah roughly out of the snowbank. Half dragging his still-dazed fellow slave, Bruin marched across to the slave quarters. The shivering guard followed unhappily, angered at being forced to leave the warm hut before he was ready.

As the Mound Builder moved the door into place behind them, Bruin began immediately to build up the fire. He spoke no word to O-Tah-Wah, who watched him angrily from the far wall of the stockade.

"So," O-Tah-Wah thought, "he is not to be trusted after all! I should have expected this. No one has ever been a friend to me before, so why should Bruin be any different?" He dropped sullenly into a peculiar, stiff-legged crouch nearer the fire. His temper was beginning to work, too. He could feel it coming on!

Suddenly, Bruin moved to the door and placed his ear against it. One huge hand motioned for silence. For a long time he stood there, listening. Finally, he turned and gave O-Tah-Wah one of his ugly, crooked grins. He reached out one hand and placed it on his small friend's shoulder.

"My angry little brother, I am truly sorry," he began. "I hope that I did not hurt you too much, but I had to act quickly. The guard saw you take the flint fragment, so I felt it best that you take your punishment from me before the Flatheads had a chance."

At that moment, O-Tah-Wah had the strangest feeling he'd ever experienced. He wanted to cry, but of course braves such as he never did. Bruin was indeed his true friend after all! O-Tah-Wah was elated. His anger was gone, and once again he felt his debt to this ugly slave who was even now cleaning the cut under his eye.

"You see," Bruin went on in a whisper, "I have been a long time making friends with the toolmaker. He can be very valuable to us. As you must know, at the time of our escape, we *must* have flint or we shall die even before we are recaptured!"

O-Tah-Wah knew Bruin was right. If they were to be successful when the spring came, every step of their plan must be perfect. The flint would be necessary for tools and weapons.

Bruin finished swabbing the cut he had made on O-Tah-Wah's face, and, grinning again, pointed to one corner of their small prison. "I have something to show you," he said. "Go into that corner and dig around in the husks. See what you find."

O-Tah-Wah did as he was told. At first he found nothing, but after a moment his probing fingers touched something hard and smooth. Flint! Eagerly, he dug deeper and was immediately rewarded by more long jagged slices of the precious stone material. He was about to shout for joy, but Bruin stopped him quickly by placing a finger to his lips and pointing to the door. They could never tell when the guard might be returning to check on them.

O-Tah-Wah placed his hands on each of Bruin's large muscular shoulders. Words failed him, for he knew that each stolen bit of stone had been taken at great risk.

After a happy, quiet moment, both men laughed. Soon they began whispering their plans for use of the eight flint blades that Bruin had been able to smuggle out of the toolmaker's house over the past weeks. Several pieces, they decided, would be broken apart for the making of arrow points. O-Tah-Wah figured that they might get as many as six small tips from the three longest blades. They would each need a knife, of course, and the remaining blades would be made into spearheads. With much luck and the favor of the Great Spirit, it now appeared that they might make a successful bid for freedom.

The short winter days seemed to fly quickly now that their plans were made. Bruin was gone a large part of each day, begging food and working for the toolmaker. O-Tah-Wah, having been thrown out for his attempted theft, did not return to the Mound Builder's house and workshop. This suited the two slaves well, however, for now O-Tah-Wah had long hours to work on the flint pieces that Bruin had so cleverly provided them.

Each day found O-Tah-Wah a little stronger than the one before. Bruin's begging skill provided him with the needed food for his healing body.

The winter was nearly over now, and several days of warmer weather had melted most of the snow. This was unfortunate for the two friends, because it brought the other slaves back to the stockade. Their return quickly ended all work on the escape weapons.

The thaw signaled the beginning of more grueling work in the forest. For Bruin and O-Tah-Wah, however, it also provided an important opportunity to get into the groves and thickets surrounding the village. There were several things that they still needed, and these were available only in the forest.

The work was very hard. Shortly after dawn each day, the slaves were marched into the woods some distance west of the mound they had worked on during the fall. O-Tah-Wah was not surprised that little progress had been made on this structure during his long illness. He could only guess at the number of hours that must still be spent at the cruel work before the mound would be finished.

Once in the pine grove, the poorly clad workers would begin clearing the brush away from the trees selected for felling. This was the hardest job of all, for the guards would allow their charges only a few tools. They feared that the slaves might use them for weapons. So the slaves tugged and twisted and tore at the bushes until the job was done. Although O-Tah-Wah hated the task of clearing, he knew that the work and cold air were exactly what he needed. His strength was now back again. This was important, for spring was coming, and with it, the time for escape.

After the clearing was completed, the workers laid a fire around each tree. The brush and sticks were placed on stones a few feet off the ground in order to burn through the tree trunk at a point thinner than the base. When the fires were lighted, all the slaves were glad, for they could easily keep the fires burning, and the heat was most welcome in the icy forest.

As darkness approached, the fires were put out. The charred wood was scraped away before the fires were relighted the next morning. Then, after several days, the trees began to fall. But the work was still far from done. Trimming the logs was the most backbreaking toil imaginable.

Whenever the slaves had a few moments to talk together, the topic was always the same: why were so many logs being cut at this time of year? With the ground frozen, there would be no way to build either houses or a temple.

Many ideas were advanced. Secretly, however, most of the slaves, including O-Tah-Wah, suspected the real reason the timbers were being prepared. Those slaves who had been working in village homes had heard the rumors. Cotauna, the high priest, was not improving. In fact, each day found him weaker than the one before. Should he die, which seemed very likely, a proper funeral must be given him. This would mean a special log death house for his remains. The structure would be burned with the body inside, and Cotauna's spirit would then ascend into the Spirit World with the smoke.

A new mound would have to be built upon the ashes. Most frightening for the slaves, however, was the knowledge that some of them would be sacrificed! Their spirits would then be available to serve Cotauna's spirit in the Next World. For O-Tah-

Wah, whose people had always worshiped the Great Spirit, the practices of these strange, intelligent people seemed especially terrible.

Bruin had guessed the truth, but he said nothing to his small friend. The giant knew that they must hurry their preparations for escape. If Cotauna died, they would make their attempt immediately. Better to die in the snow than be killed as part of the Flatheads' funeral ceremony!

In view of these developments, Bruin began taking great risks to secure the materials they needed. The smaller items were easy enough to hide in his clothing or in an armpit. But the long pieces were more of a problem. How could he and O-Tah-Wah carry the sticks and tree limbs that would become spear shafts, bows, and arrows? The Lazy One solved their problem. Due to the bad knee, O-Tah-Wah always walked stiff-legged. It was therefore a simple matter to slip the long branches inside his leggings, where they rode along right into the stockade. Once inside, the two scheming slaves buried everything under the husk floor. So far, they had managed to keep their secret from the other slaves, but the risk of discovery grew greater with every new object.

The most difficult problem was finding time to scrape down the rough shafts without the others finding out. The two slaves had but one choice. They were forced to work in darkness, late at night when the others were sleeping. But Bruin knew that this method was too slow. One evening as they trudged back to the stockade, he spoke with O-Tah-Wah about it.

"Little brother," he whispered, "I think it would be wise if you were to become sick again."

Limping carefully, so as not to give away the arrow shaft riding next to the Lazy One, O-Tah-Wah answered quietly. "I have been thinking the same thing. I could get much work done while the others are busy in the grove."

"You must begin pretending tomorrow." Bruin urged him. "If the plan works and you are left alone, be very careful. The guards will certainly check on you often. No doubt they will also kick and beat you in order to see if you are really sick." Bruin slowed his pace a little. When O-Tah-Wah was very close, the giant whispered urgently, "You will have to control your anger now, for should you allow them to taunt you into striking back or even giving them an angry look, all will be lost!"

O-Tah-Wah dropped behind the others. They were nearing the stockade. By now it seemed much more like a home to him than a prison. He was thinking of what Bruin had just said. His temper—could he really control it? Or would it be the cause of their undoing? Clamping his jaw rigidly, he crawled into the foul-smelling prison. The coming days would provide the answer.

CHAPTER 7

The Journey to Blessed Mountain

The night passed as if it had never been. O-Tah-Wah had planned to start pretending sickness before morning, but he had not been able to waken himself early enough. Now a loud shouting arose outside the stockade.

Many men could be heard talking and moving about beyond the walls. The slaves were worried. What could this mean? The door opened, letting in cold along with the uneasy light of morning. O-Tah-Wah forgot all about playing sick as he saw the toolmaker entering the slave quarters.

The fat little man wrinkled his nose in distaste as he peered about at the frightened forms crouching here and there in the darkness. Two warriors joined him in the stockade and he began giving orders. "We need all who can do a full day's work," he began. "Each one who is chosen will dress warmly and prepare for a five-day march. We go to Blessed Mountain for flint. My supply is nearly gone, and many more arrows will soon be needed for the spring hunting." He gave the two guards more instructions, then turned and waddled quickly into the sunlight. The smell in the prison was very bad. "Be sure," he shouted through the doorway, "that you select the Big One and his angry friend. These two are worth six of the rest. Also, the Big One will watch to see that no flint is stolen by the others!"

O-Tah-Wah looked helplessly at Bruin. Now their plans would have to wait once again. The giant only shrugged, for there was no way to avoid going. "Perhaps," he whispered to O-Tah-Wah as he wrapped his body with some miserably worn-out skins, "we may learn something about the country that will be useful in our escape."

"Have you been to this place before?"

"Yes," Bruin grunted. Glancing around, the giant saw that the warriors were busy selecting other slaves for the journey. "Four years ago, I made this journey with over 100 slaves from many villages. I cannot tell you how many bags of flint we brought back, but it was a very great number. The Flatheads use flint for everything. Much of it they trade, but of course you know this."

The Mound Builders herded the chosen slaves out of the stockade. Several of the slaves had not been able to finish wrapping themselves with skins. The cold would soon deal cruelly with them. The toolmaker and his companions, on the other hand, were beautifully dressed. Their moosehide footwear was warm and nearly waterproof and their buckskin shirts and trousers were lined with soft fur of rabbit and fox. O-Tah-Wah stared bitterly at his captors. He had been able to finish dressing, but even so, he was already very cold.

Despite his anger at the unfair treatment, O-Tah-Wah could not help admiring the clever workmanship on the clothing of the Mound Builders. "Probably," he thought as the workers started out of the village, "they have certain members of the tribe who do not hunt, or work flint, or raise corn, but who only cut and sew skins." The idea was most interesting to him, and for the moment, thinking about it helped him forget the cold. The idea was well fixed in his brain, however. Once again, he found himself thinking of ways by which he might share this knowledge with his own people.

Leaving the village, the small band headed northwest, following a well-marked trail. Bruin stayed near O-Tah-Wah as they marched, and several times knowing looks were exchanged as they observed certain features of the countryside. Thickets that would provide good cover and caves that would provide shelter were carefully noted. If their escape route took them through this country, such knowledge could be very useful to them.

The Lazy One was beginning to tire when they stopped for food and a midday rest. Bruin eyed O-Tah-Wah quietly as they ate. He could see that the young hunter was having trouble. The big slave hoped that the Flatheads would not notice. If they did, it was certain they would begin to taunt O-Tah-Wah, and Bruin knew well how the hot-tempered O-Tah-Wah reacted to such treatment.

When they moved on, however, O-Tah-Wah seemed rested and able to limp along fairly well again. Bruin, watching his small friend stumping bravely along ahead of him, began to feel what was, for him, a new emotion. It was hatred. One mighty fist closed steadily on the thick, smooth shaft of the hammer he carried. Never in his life had Bruin felt quite this way. No one deserved the treatment O-Tah-Wah had been given. "I will repay these Flatheads for their cruelty," he thought coldly. The knuckles of his right hand were white with the pressure of his grip, and the muscles in his forearm were aching with tension. O-Tah-Wah could not have known how loyal this man was. His first friend was a fine one indeed!

They traveled on, across the rolling, snow-softened hills, following a series of connected trails that became straighter and wider with every passing mile. O-Tah-Wah could see that, over the years, many feet had passed this way. This was not surprising, for if what Bruin said was true, the paths led to a great treasure: an actual mountain of the finest quality flint to be found anywhere in the world. O-Tah-Wah had seen some of it on weapons carried by the priests and chiefs. Even the common people of the village sometimes used it. With envy, O-Tah-Wah remembered how easily the toolmaker had chipped the glossy stone. In a few hours, the broken hunks had been fashioned into weapons and tools that were masterpieces of design and beauty. It was the quality of the flint found on Blessed Mountain that had made such workmanship possible.

The fat little toolmaker had been very anxious to get an early start, but he tired quickly. It was still early in the afternoon when commands were given for a halt. Puffing and blowing, the toolmaker plopped himself down beside a clump of sumac and ordered a fire made. Food was made ready for him, and he ate large quantities of it, smacking his lips and beaming round-faced smiles at everyone who looked his way. Even the slaves received kindly glances. The toolmaker was a friend to all, as long as his belly was full.

The slaves built their own fire, but no food was offered them. The guards would give them a few handfuls of cornmeal before dark and maybe throw them any bones or scraps left from their own dinner. But O-Tah-Wah didn't care. He was grateful for the early halt. The Lazy One was nearing the end of its endurance, and the young hunter did not wish to let the Flatheads know how tired he was.

Bruin watched O-Tah-Wah, noting calmly the drops of sweat that made several crooked streaks down each side of his face.

Bruin saw also the rapidly heaving chest and open mouth. He was not fooled. O-Tah-Wah was near the point of total exhaustion. This was not good. Escape would mean much faster and longer travel than this! The giant was not greatly worried, however. For Bruin saw in his friend great courage, and even more than courage, high spirit and a sense of self-pride. These qualities would do much to make up for a physical disability. "He will do," Bruin thought to himself. "Yes, when our time of testing comes, he will do very well."

The slaves had work to do, of course, but gathering firewood and building the crude, quick shelters was light duty compared with the work they were used to doing. As darkness fell over the little valley, their work was done.

For the first time in many weeks, O-Tah-Wah felt really warm. The Mound Builders had brought several thick bearskin robes. To the slave's surprise, the Mound Builders readily shared these skins. O-Tah-Wah had one all to himself. Rolled up in the fragrant fur, he felt safe and well. Snowflakes began to fall in the silent, motionless moments of a short winter twilight. The fire near his feet flickered bravely, doing its best to keep back the darkness that moved slowly but steadily closer.

O-Tah-Wah was very tired. His own body quickly heated the little cocoon to a drowsy warmth, and very soon he was sleeping.

In what seemed like a moment, night was gone and the young hunter found himself being kicked awake by one of the Flathead warriors. Today's march would bring them to the ridge of flint they were seeking.

The night's rest had helped, and O-Tah-Wah was having less trouble keeping up. Shortly after the midday rest, there came a sudden, soft command to halt. O-Tah-Wah looked at Bruin, but the giant only shrugged. Suddenly, the Mound Builders began to take cover behind trees and logs, fitting arrows to their bowstrings as they ran. Seeing this, Bruin pushed O-Tah-Wah off the trail. They crouched down in the snow behind a low, dirt bank. Here they lay quietly, listening for some indication of what might be going on. O-Tah-Wah's keen ear soon caught the soft rustlings of men moving in the forest.

Several moments passed, and then the two slaves heard voices. The language was unknown to them, but the sounds seemed friendly. When a few of the Mound Builders began moving cautiously back toward the trail, O-Tah-Wah and Bruin arose and looked over the bank. Lined up along a large clearing was a party of 20 or 30 warriors! They were dressed like no one O-Tah-Wah had ever seen before.

O-Tah-Wah noticed that these men also had their weapons ready. Their headman appeared to be unarmed, however. He was trying to talk with the toolmaker in sign language. After a few minutes, both tribes respectfully backed away from each other and went their separate ways.

"What happened?" O-Tah-Wah asked when they were on the move again. "They were stronger than we, and heavily armed. Why did they not attack, or at least force us to pay them tribute?"

"We are nearing the Blessed Mountain," Bruin replied. "Long, long ago, it was agreed that never would any people make war upon any other when in the Land of Flint. It was a very wise decision, for what tribe could long survive without good stone for arrows, knives, and spears?"

O-Tah-Wah nodded. Men of much wisdom must have sat long in the council houses to arrive at a good rule such as this. He wondered why these same great leaders had not made rules against slavery!

The ridge they were approaching looked no different from

any other at first. But as they climbed higher, O-Tah-Wah began to notice outcroppings of flint here and there along the trail. The excitement shown by the Mound Builders was increasing, too. They were now walking upon Blessed Mountain!

Several times O-Tah-Wah heard the sound of hammers near the spine of the ridge. "Others must be here before us," he thought as he struggled up the steep path. "Perhaps they will not remember the rule of 'no warfare.' Maybe these tribesmen have never heard the decision." He was a little frightened, but the Flatheads seemed unconcerned. They climbed steadily upward, making no effort to keep silent. Watching them, O-Tah-Wah relaxed a little and concentrated on the painful task of dragging the Lazy One up the slope.

On top, the entire party stopped in a group, looking about them at the surprising sights that everywhere met their gaze. Large piles of dirt dotted the half-cleared ridge. Beside each one, a deep pit had been gouged out of the mountain. Work crews had cleared away the soil to get at the finest quality flint, which usually lay six to eight feet below the surface. Here and there, men could be seen at work, and the ring of stone hammers upon the exposed rock made a steady, musical sound.

The fat toolmaker hurried about, smiling and talking. He had decided that they should set up camp at once. Then it would be possible to begin the first day's work before sundown. While the slaves and their guards rested, the little man waddled importantly along the ridge, peering into abandoned pits, examining rock samples, and scratching at the frozen dirt in various places. It was plain to see that the man loved his work. He was excited at the prospect of so much fine stone just waiting to be taken.

O-Tah-Wah nodded as he watched. This was the Mound Builders' strong point. Each person had a special job that he was to learn. It was easy to see how such a man as the toolmaker could know so much about flint and how to fashion it. Making tools was all he had to do! O-Tah-Wah nodded again. "I will remember this lesson when I am free," he thought, still watching the busy man's progress.

The toolmaker finally selected the site for digging. O-Tah-Wah, Bruin, and two other slaves were put to work at once, clearing weeds and brush away from the edges of the pit.

It was easy to see why the round little man had chosen this pit rather than any of the others. The flint ledge of the pit was not as far down, and it appeared to be of excellent quality. Even the slaves became excited at the sight of the shiny layers of smooth blue-and-brown stone showing plainly between the patches of snow.

One problem stood in the way of an immediate beginning. Whoever had first opened this pit had stopped digging on the eastern wall because of two shag-bark hickory trees. They had followed the flint vein up to the trees' roots but then had been forced to quit. No doubt, they were afraid the trees might fall on them if they weakened the roots by more digging.

The toolmaker was not stupid. He had quickly determined that the very best flint probably lay under the nut trees. Getting at the flint presented a problem, but the tookmaker saw it as an opportunity instead. The clever plan he devised was this: he would pull the trees down first; as they fell into the pit, their roots would lift a large part of the earth, tearing it loose and exposing the new flint all at once!

O-Tah-Wah did not grasp the idea at first, but Bruin soon caught on. The giant explained the work to his friend as they dug under the roots, weakening the trees even further.

Large ropes of braided rawhide were tied to the trunks 20 feet above ground. When all of the slaves were out of the pit, the entire party began to pull on the ropes. They did not tug hard but set up a rhythm: pull—release, pull—release, pull—release. The trees began to sway, slowly at first, then faster and faster. The weights of the trunks themselves helped loosen the roots' hold on the soil, and in a surprisingly short time, the trees began to fall. Slaves and Flatheads alike dashed out of the way as the hickories came crashing to the ground. As the toolmaker had hoped, their intertwined roots had lifted several tons of earth. Getting to the new flint would be simple now!

The early winter darkness was on its way by the time the trees had been pulled over. The toolmaker posted a guard for each part of the night. So far, the other groups at work up and down the ten-mile ridge had ignored them. Still, as leader of the expedition, he was naturally cautious.

At dawn, the toolmaker was already up. His enthusiasm spread throughout the camp. Several slaves were smiling and talking together. Their guards were not so strict and allowed a little more freedom than usual. Even O-Tah-Wah, who was usually angry and sullen, felt a painful twinge of happiness on this bright, snow-sparkled morning.

Coals from the night's fire were poked and blown upon. Dry sticks added to glowing embers burst noisily into flame. The fire, however, would have to be much larger than this before they were through.

It took the greater part of the day to clear the new flint vein of remaining earth. The slaves were kept busy every minute. While two scraped and chopped at the frosty soil, others dragged out the loose material. Slaves and guards at the rim loaded the larger clods onto skins that were spread out near the new pit. When the hides were covered, two men would drag them out of the way and dump the load. By noon, their digging sticks were glancing off the slippery surface of a fine vein of pure flint. The toolmaker had been right, as usual.

The little craftsman was going crazy! Bruin watched him in absolute amazement. The man simply could not wait to get the beautiful stone out of the ground. The guards shook their heads, grinning at each other whenever they were sure their leader could not see them. At last, as the toolmaker leaned far over the pit, trying to get a better look at the face of the rock, his foot slipped sidewise. Down he went, bouncing off the edges and scraping his fat belly on the pit wall as he fell. He landed against the stone on the bottom of the hole. As he scrambled to his feet, slipping and sliding on the bad footing, he moved one hand soothingly over the stone. For a moment, he thought he had *hurt* it! Laughter rang out from all sides of the pit. No one could help it.

The toolmaker didn't seem to mind. Nothing could make him unhappy today. Grinning foolishly, he allowed himself to be helped out of the hole. His beautiful, fur-lined shirt was torn and muddy, and the exposed stomach was badly scraped. On his face, however, was the smile of a happy child.

O-Tah-Wah smiled, too, although he did not laugh aloud, as did the others. "This fat one, this toolmaker," he mused, "seems to be a good man. Many of the Flatheads are kind, as well. Why is it, then, that they keep us here against our will?" There was no answer. The others continued to chuckle, but already O-Tah-Wah's smile was gone. He could not laugh and have fun with people who had robbed him of the only thing of value that he owned—his freedom.

They prepared for the night early, but after their evening meal, the toolmaker surprised everyone by ordering more work. He wanted a fire laid in the new pit. The wood was to be placed directly against the exposed flint vein.

The slaves had no help with this task. Their guards, tired and cold, stayed near the cooking fires and watched them work.

Small tree limbs and brush were piled in the pit first. On top of these were placed larger logs. All of the wood was piled tightly against the stone. The toolmaker wanted the rock to be red-hot by morning.

When one side of the pit was nearly full, they set the wood ablaze. Several of the guards moved their sleeping skins nearer the pit to see that the slaves continued to feed the fire all through the night.

O-Tah-Wah was given the first duty. This was good, for as soon as his watch was over, he would be able to roll up in the warm robe and sleep until morning. He was very tired, but wood was lying everywhere around the pit and there was not much work in gathering it. Heat from the roaring flames rolled upward with the sparks into the winter sky. O-Tah-Wah liked to watch the smoke as it rose, lighted eerily by the firelight below. The crippled slave envied the ease with which it rose from the earth, over the trees, and away into the heavens. If only he were able to fly as the smoke did!

In a few hours, O-Tah-Wah was relieved by another slave. The fire was burning harder than ever by now. The pit's bottom shimmered with a yellow-orange brilliance glowing from a deep bed of fiery embers. Snow had melted for a good distance around the rim of the pit, and wispy tails of steam rose gently from the thawing earth.

Exhausted, O-Tah-Wah rolled up in his borrowed bearskin robe. The last thing he remembered before falling asleep was a great shower of sparks that burst out of the pit as a new log was thrown on the coals.

Once again, morning did not dawn quickly enough for the toolmaker. After inspecting the fire, he roused the camp. Very soon, all of the men were hard at work. Bruin did not know what the little man had in mind this time, but he was sure it would be clever.

Two slaves were sent into the surrounding forest to cut three long poles. The rest of the slaves and guards began to gather snow, piling it on skins that they pulled along behind them. The toolmaker kept everyone busy, but no one seemed to mind working for him.

When the poles had been dragged near the little quarry, they were lashed together at one end. A large skin was then tied between the poles a few feet below the point at which they were joined. The bag was packed full of snow. Now the men raised the huge tripod, setting the stout legs well back from the fire's heat. The bag of snow swung gently back and forth just above the shimmering pit.

The flames had been allowed to die down while the snow bag was being erected. There was nothing to do now but wait. The toolmaker ordered food for everyone even though it was only mid-morning. They sat around the pit, guards and slaves alike, enjoying the generosity shown by their leader.

As the rising heat melted the snow in the swaying skin sack, O-Tah-Wah and Bruin argued about the reason it had been hung in this position. They did not have long to wonder, however. The toolmaker, who had been studying the fire for some time, clapped his hands to summon his helpers. Working rapidly with long sticks and branches, they raked the hot coals away from the flint. When the stone was completely exposed, he squinted up at the bag of snow water above them. After moving a few feet and studying the bag again, several men were ordered to slide one of the tripod's legs a few feet farther from the pit. This brought the water directly over the flint. The toolmaker took one last look at the bag's position, then grasped a rawhide rope that was fastened to one side of the bag. With a quick jerk, he broke the supporting thongs. The cold water burst from the sack and plunged down in a thick sheet directly onto the red-hot flint. Steam boiled up all around, hiding the men from each other. It was impossible to see into the pit at all, but it was not necessary. They could all hear what was going on! Sharp crackling and snapping sounds told them that the icy water was causing the heated stone to split and shatter into hundreds of smaller pieces. Now they need only let the stone cool and gather up the fragments. O-Tah-Wah and Bruin shook their heads. The Mound Builders continually amazed them.

CHAPTER 8

The Death of Cotauna

The fires in the log temple were roaring. The heat was so intense that several of the young priests were gleaming with sweat. Their chanting had been going on since sundown, six hours before. Smoke was so thick within the walls that even the bright light from the fires hardly reached the far corners of the hall. The chanting softly rose and fell from the rows of minor priests seated behind a skin-covered platform.

The high priest Cotauna lay unmoving on a special bed prepared for him in the center of the temple. His eyes were closed, and only the slight rise and fall of his chest proved that life still remained in his body.

Little Eyes, older and wiser since his encounter with Turtle Shell, was glad he had given orders months ago to start the logging operation. He had expected that the old priest's funeral would be held soon. Therefore, the timbers had been cut for Cotauna's death house. The high priest had lived a long time. He had once told Little Eyes that he could remember more than 60 winters! Certainly, it seemed to many of the villagers that Cotauna had been their high priest forever.

Little Eyes rose to his feet and moved slowly across the smoky room to Cotauna's side. His shadow rippled along the log walls behind him, finally blending in with those of the seated chanters. Little Eyes' face was still handsome, but many lines and wrinkles now showed around his forehead. He folded his arms under the beautifully decorated elk-hide robe. Soberly, Little Eyes watched the medicine man whose fierce, wolf-like mask was terrible to see. The firelight, flickering and glittering about the medicine man seemed to make his body appear even more like the animal he was imitating. Little Eyes took no part, but only watched as the medicine man performed a healing ritual over Cotauna's body.

Another priest now joined them. He was smoking a ceremonial stone pipe. The small object was carved of slate in the likeness of an otter, Cotauna's personal totem. Drawing deeply on the stem, the priest then exhaled the fragrant vapors in a soft cloud under Cotauna's nostrils. Magic mumblings accompanied the smoke, but as before, the old priest did not respond. Cotauna was dying.

Little Eyes gazed quietly at the form of the tribe's religious leader. Many thoughts passed through his mind as he watched the old man grow weaker and weaker with each passing hour. Who would be able to take this man's place in the village? How would he, Little Eyes, be looked upon when Cotauna was no longer here to command the respect of the people? Would he become the highest ruler of the tribe? Little Eyes' face gave no hint of the questions he felt inside. This was good, for there were no answers to them.

The sun was rising in the east when the dreaded moment came. With a long, tired-sounding sigh, Cotauna's spirit left his worn-out body. Most of the priests and nobles present recognized the sound immediately. The low chanting was quickly hushed. For some moments, there was no sound at all in the smoky hall. When many careful examinations had been made, and it was certain that Cotauna was indeed dead, the death wail was begun.

Many of those who had been waiting for the end now left the temple. Little Eyes left, too, drawing his official robes closer as his sweating body met the shocking cold of the late winter morning. In a matter of minutes, everyone in the village would know of the loss of their respected priest Cotauna. There was much work to be done.

Little Eyes hurried to his own house to put on more clothes. He would personally be directing the slaves' activities for the next few days.

Warmly dressed in a winter robe made of the white-skinned snowshoe rabbit, the chief headed for the slave hut. His servants hurried before him, clearing the melting snow from his path. Little Eyes paid no attention to them. They received no thanks, and in fact were ignored entirely. These men were lucky to have such an honored position as that of servant to the chief. This position was thanks enough.

The slaves had not yet left for the forest when Little Eyes arrived. Several were still eating the corn mush they had been given for their morning meal. The men made a pitiful sight, standing in the cold morning light, shivering and rubbing their red, scratched legs for warmth. The chief's sudden appearance in the slave quarters struck instant terror into their hearts.

Bruin and O-Tah-Wah, eating together as usual, stood perfectly still. The slaves had heard the rumors about Cotauna's illness. Each one realized what Little Eyes' visit meant. A great priest such as Cotauna would need many servants and slaves in the Spirit World. Yes, they feared that soon all but the luckiest of them would be with the religious leader of the Flatheads, and that before many days had passed, their own bodies would form the beginning of yet another mound. They had good reason to be sick with dread.

Little Eyes did not speak directly to the slaves, for it would not be proper at a time such as this. Instead, he gave his orders to one of the guards. The guard then growled instructions to the frightened little group before him.

The first job was snaking the logs to the area chosen for the new mound. The melting snow would make this task somewhat easier than it would have been during the dead of winter. Had Cotauna's death come earlier, the slaves would have been forced to wait for his burial. It was now close enough to spring to hold the ceremony, even though it would be difficult.

O-Tah-Wah's mind was racing. He and Bruin were not nearly ready to attempt an escape. The crippled hunter knew, however, that there would be no chance to wait for the warm rains of spring now.

Bruin had been sent to another work group where his strength was needed. But before he left, the big slave had explained the building procedure that was to occur during the coming days.

First, it would be necessary to clear a large circle of earth as a base for Cotauna's mound. The snow would be scraped away and all sticks and stones removed. Then, fires would be kept burning for two days and nights on the cleared circle. When the clay was baked hard and the ashes swept away, Cotauna's burial chamber of logs would be built in the center of this cleared area. His body, and those of his slaves and servants, would be placed there with all his personal possessions. A larger log temple would next be erected over the tomb. Finally, after much ceremony and ritual, the whole structure would be set ablaze. In spring, the undisturbed ashes would be covered with a layer of earth. Many, many more layers would be added over a period of years until Cotauna's mound was built. This monument to the respected Flathead leader would stand for 3,000 years, and more!

O-Tah-Wah felt quite sure that no slaves would be killed until the timbers were in place and the hard work of clearing was finished. This meant that he and Bruin might have another four days to prepare for their escape.

The Lazy One was aching, as usual, and O-Tah-Wah was becoming very angry, as usual. Everything was going wrong. If only Cotauna would have remained alive until the Month of Forest Flowers. Even the Month of Much Rain would have helped. Rage was not unknown to O-Tah-Wah, and now he found it to be his companion yet again. Furiously, he yanked on the braided rawhide rope that drew the log steadily toward the village. His temper gave him a strength beyond anything the other four slaves in his group thought possible. The log bumped and slithered rapidly along over the brush and melting drifts of snow.

O-Tah-Wah's companions were too numb with thoughts of their impending death to notice how the work was going. Several were so frightened that they were unable to work at all. The guards set upon them with clubs and whips. The beatings forced the poor creatures to begin working, but it was plain that they hardly knew what was happening to them.

By late afternoon, a respectable pile of logs was growing beside the high, level riverbank that had been chosen as Cotauna's final resting place. A large number of men and women from the village had nearly finished the clearing operation. In fact, several of the Flatheads had already begun carrying in dry brush.

This would be burned first to thaw the ground. It would then be easier to dig the necessary post holes for the walls of Cotauna's death house.

O-Tah-Wah was alarmed at how rapidly the work was progressing. He must tell Bruin of what had been done already on this, the very first day after Cotauna's death! Perhaps now, they would only have three days before they must escape. Anger burned within him. The crippled slave made no attempt to control his temper. Bruin had warned him of this, but O-Tah-Wah forgot the words. Rather than using every minute to plan the details of their flight, O-Tah-Wah was selfishly allowing himself the pleasure of hating everything: the Flatheads, the aching Lazy One, and the dead priest Cotauna.

As the darkness closed in, O-Tah-Wah anxiously began watching for Bruin's crew. At last he saw the giant, trudging along toward the stockade with four others. Bruin was not hard to pick out, for he stood almost a head taller than the others.

O-Tah-Wah's group was soon allowed to quit working, too, and he hurried as fast as the guard would allow. Still, he was unable to catch up with Bruin's crew until they arrived at the stockade. It seemed forever until the other slaves were finally sleeping, and the two plotters could begin their nightly whispering session. They had finished an amazing amount of work in this way during the past few weeks. Many of their tools, spears, and arrows had been fashioned by touch alone. They had even managed a short bow. The weapons were crude in comparison with the beautifully finished articles made by the Mound Builders. But Bruin and O-Tah-Wah hoped their weapons would serve until they had traveled far enough to risk making more. These weapons would be good enough for killing game, but the slaves hoped they would not have to use them for self-defense. Both Bruin and O-Tah-Wah feared that in a fight, they would not stand much of a chance with these homemade articles. Although O-Tah-Wah hated the Flatheads for their cruel practices and for their use of slaves, he still respected their skill. With these people rested the greatest power O-Tah-Wah could possibly imagine.

O-Tah-Wah began whispering to his friend. First he told Bruin of the rapid progress that was being made on Cotauna's burial site. O-Tah-Wah was still angry, and his words came out in explosive, popping sounds. Bruin said very little. After some time, as O-Tah-Wah was finishing his account, the crippled slave began noticing how quiet his friend seemed to be. At last he asked the reason.

"My angry little friend," Bruin began, "I think you are right that time is shorter than we had expected. This does not concern me, however. My thoughts this night rest with the others who sleep as we prepare for our escape. It is my feeling that they should be told of our plans. Yes, it is my thought that our fellow slaves should be given the chance to escape with us."

"*What*?" O-Tah-Wah was furious! His whisper was almost a shout. "You would ask these cowards, these *rabbits* who call themselves men, to make an escape with us? Surely, the Hunger Moon has robbed you of the little wisdom you once had!"

"You know as well as I," he continued in a hissing whisper, "that not one among them has the courage to try, much less ever really make an escape!"

Bruin's reply was calm, as usual. "Perhaps you are right. Still, I cannot leave this prison without offering them a chance to come along."

"But they have made no preparations!" O-Tah-Wah could hardly believe that this was happening. It was madness! A miracle would be necessary even for the two of them to stay ahead of the powerful Flathead search parties. More than two runaways would be sure to leave a trail that the dogs and trackers simply could not miss. O-Tah-Wah's blood was boiling.

Bruin, however, ignored the childish anger O-Tah-Wah displayed. The giant had been planning all day. No temper tantrums clouded *his* mind. As he worked, he had been thinking. "Suppose," he began, "that some of the others would wish to try? And suppose, also, that after traveling together for awhile, some of them were to strike off in a different direction? Would this not improve the chances for all of us?"

O-Tah-Wah's anger faded like fog in the morning sun. Immediately, he saw the wisdom of the plan. The plan might make it possible for some of them to actually succeed in their try for freedom. He did not take time to apologize, for he was too busy kicking the other slaves awake. Bruin shook with silent laughter.

Six of the others agreed to try. Bruin had built up the fire, and the flickering shadows danced around the cold log walls like evil spirits seeking a home. Whispered conversation went on and on through the night, and by morning the escape plan was set.

The main problem was that all of the slaves wished to head north. This was hardly surprising, since north was the direction closest to freedom. After much anxious haggling, O-Tah-Wah had solved the problem by suggesting that lots be cast to determine the route each pair would take. He and Bruin had drawn the northeast route. They could not have been happier, for this was very nearly the direction they had planned to take, anyway.

Bruin insisted that the few weapons they had be shared. O-Tah-Wah argued furiously against this. But he finally agreed when Bruin pointed out that now *all* the slaves could work on making weapons and tools. It would no longer be necessary to work in darkness.

They set the escape for two nights later. The slaves were excited and almost happy now. For years they had merely existed, letting each day blend into the next. They had no hope, no plans—nothing! But *now*, even though every one of them expected to be caught and killed or even tortured to death, they felt like real men again. Like the trader Turtle Shell, whom most of them had known, they felt a certain pride in trying to cheat the Flatheads of their terrible plans.

O-Tah-Wah could not sleep, even though his body was exhausted from a full day's work and the strain of planning. Feverishly, he scraped down the shaft of his spear. The small flint tool, made in the shape of the new moon, worked very well. Each stroke of the curved blade took off a little more of the roughness and brought the handle into truer balance. The flint chip he was using could have been made into an arrow point, but used as a scraper, it was a very necessary tool. As badly as they needed flint for weapons, they could not do without the scraper.

Bruin curled up in his usual spot near the fire. He appeared to be sleeping, but O-Tah-Wah knew he was only resting. In fact, O-Tah-Wah was quite sure that none of the slaves were sleeping. It made little difference, anyway, for dawn was very near.

CHAPTER 9

O-Tah-Wah Makes a Bargain

O-Tah-Wah was awakened by the sound of the log door being opened. He was surprised that he had been able to sleep at all, even for an hour or two. There was no time to be spent in wondering, however, for the small prison was rapidly filling up with people. O-Tah-Wah scooted his body next to Bruin's and, heart pounding, asked the giant what this might mean. Bruin never got a chance to answer, for Little Eyes had entered.

The chief looked slowly around at the ugly little prison. His distaste for the dirt and the smell was evident by his frown. The great man seemed in no hurry, but after a keen look at each slave, he began to speak. As usual, his remarks were directed to one of his warriors who repeated them to the captives.

"As slaves of the Mound Builders, you have indeed been most fortunate. It has been your privilege to serve us, for ours is the greatest nation upon the entire earth!" Little Eyes paused, his eyes moving swiftly from face to face. He was trying to tell what effect his words were having on the miserable lot before him.

"For your labors," he continued, "we have given you food and clothing, and also a place to sleep."

The slaves were standing along the log walls. They did not move or speak. Several of them stared steadily at the ground. But O-Tah-Wah was not one of these. His black eyes snapped and glittered under their heavy brows. Fury caused the veins in his neck to swell and protrude. Bruin saw the signs. One huge hand moved slowly to O-Tah-Wah's elbow. The fingers circled his arm and began to close with a steady, crushing pressure. The crippled slave was hardly aware of the hint at first, but Bruin's grip was such that no one could ignore it for long. O-Tah-Wah finally got the silent signal and tried to hide his anger.

Bruin could not tell if Little Eyes had seen all of this or not. If he had, no sign was given. The chief began speaking again. "Now a great honor is awaiting five of you. Those who are chosen will be made ready, and when the right moment comes, your spirits will join that of Cotauna, our departed leader. It will be your duty to serve him in the Spirit World. It would not do for him to walk on the Winds of the Morning without servants to attend him!"

O-Tah-Wah's brain was throbbing with hate. Only five were to be taken as sacrifices. What now of their careful plans? The crippled hunter knew that each one would try to make sure that it was he who would be left alive! In fact, one of them might even tell the guards of the escape plan, hoping that by doing so, he would gain favor and not be chosen to die. "This Little Eyes," O-Tah-Wah thought bitterly, "has grown a great deal wiser since the days of the trader Turtle Shell!"

Little Eyes now nodded to one of the priests who had entered the stockade earlier. The priest made his selection calmly and without hesitation. O-Tah-Wah and four others were chosen.

Bruin was not among them.

O-Tah-Wah moved as if in a dream. His mind could hardly accept what was happening as he and the other four chosen slaves were hurried to the temple. What was to become of them? How could he get a message to Bruin, his faithful friend? Should he try to break free now, this very minute? These and other thoughts whirled around in O-Tah-Wah's brain as he marched across the slushy patches of snow toward the home of the priests.

Although he had not been back to the temple since shortly after his capture, O-Tah-Wah remembered well the inside of the huge log building. Angrily, he peered from one face to another. The minor priests looked back at the five ragged, dirty slaves huddled before them. They stared longest at O-Tah-Wah. Like Cotauna and the priests of other Mound Builders, they had been taught that persons who were deformed or otherwise abnormal were special. They believed that such people often had supernatural powers. The priestly group also stared at O-Tah-Wah because of the obvious hate and fury in his eyes.

The priests set to work immediately. O-Tah-Wah and the others were stripped of their ragged clothing and scrubbed down with snow water. The shivering men were then ordered to rub themselves with bear grease until their bodies shone in the firelight. Once more O-Tah-Wah held their attention. Thanks to Bruin's care, the young slave was in perfect condition. Although he was still quite thin, his muscles were hard and strong. His long black hair, now clean and shining with grease, had been knotted carefully on top of his head in the style of the Mound Builders. And the Lazy One, ugly by O-Tah-Wah's standards, was considered a mark of real beauty by the Mound Builders. In fact, the young priests felt that if this man had been born of the Mound Builder tribe, had had his head flattened, and had been tatooed on the face and chest, he would have been as handsome as any of them.

O-Tah-Wah was forcing himself to think, for he knew that time was running out for him. Still, he had learned from the priests' talk that the funeral pyre would not be lighted until sundown the following day. O-Tah-Wah tried hard to think of what he must do. How he longed for the wisdom of his friend, Bruin. "Where is Bruin now?" he wondered sadly. "Will he be allowed to live this time, only to be chosen when another chief or priest dies?" O-Tah-Wah did not know, but the ache of loneliness was even worse than the fear in his heart.

Little Eyes, flanked by six of the tribe's finest warriors, sat unmoving near the door. O-Tah-Wah's gaze constantly returned to the chief. Bruin's story of Turtle Shell came back to him, too, but O-Tah-Wah could think of no such clever plan as the trader had used.

O-Tah-Wah looked down bitterly at the beautiful doeskin leggings that were being fitted to his body. How he had longed for some warm, soft clothing during those endless winter months when he had lain sick and freezing in the wretched stockade. Now he was being dressed well just so he could be put to death. "This," O-Tah-Wah snarled to himself, "is the way with these people. Everything fine is done for them only after they are *dead*! Turtle Shell had been right about these people and their foolish customs."

It was one of the priests himself who finally gave O-Tah-Wah the idea he had been so desperately seeking. The young priest's name was Eagle Wing. Like the other priests, he was anxious that Cotauna have a proper funeral—one befitting a man of such great age. "You are the slave who was visited by Cotauna?" he asked casually as he painted fake tattoos on O-Tah-Wah's face. He kept on with his work as he waited for the slave's reply.

"Yes, the great one came to the stockade on an evening in autumn," O-Tah-Wah answered. His mind was racing. A plan was coming! Almost before he had time to think, the words were out of his mouth. "I have been wondering how long it would be until someone here asked me of Cotauna's request." Eagle Wing stopped painting very quickly.

"Request?" he asked in surprise. "What request?"

"Perhaps I have said too much," O-Tah-Wah growled, and he spoke no more.

Eagle Wing resumed his painting, but O-Tah-Wah noticed that now he was working more slowly. "Feel free to tell me what was asked of you," he said. Eagle Wing's tone was very friendly, and O-Tah-Wah saw that the priest had lowered his voice so the others could not hear.

"No," O-Tah-Wah said sadly, "I cannot say more, for it is plain that Cotauna's words were not meant for your ears." Eagle Wing tried to seem uninterested. In fact, he even stopped working and walked away. After a few minutes, however, O-Tah-Wah was secretly delighted to see him circling back again. In his hand was a good-sized chunk of roasted venison. The man appeared to be eating the meat, but he was really only nibbling at it.

"I have always pitied you slaves," he began, his voice hardly more than a whisper. "Why don't you eat some of this meat, and as you do, you can tell me of Cotauna's visit and this special 'request' you have spoken of. Do not worry about the others. If they ask why you have been given food, I shall tell them."

"This is a kindly act you have done," O-Tah-Wah mumbled, his mouth crammed with venison. "I have always felt sorry for you priests, too, for it seems to me that you are part of an even greater slavery than we are." O-Tah-Wah was slurping and gobbling the food in a frenzy, for he guessed that it would soon be taken away from him, and he wanted to eat as much of it as possible. The rich, fat meat would give him strength for his escape.

"What do you mean by this foul talk?" Eagle Wing snapped. His friendly manner was gone now, but so was almost a pound of venison. "How can you, who are about to die, feel sorry for *us*? We are the priests of the greatest tribe on the earth, and you, a *slave*, say that you feel sorry for us! It is the talk of a madman!"

O-Tah-Wah smiled his nicest and most kindly smile. As he did so, he felt a wild surge of joy. He had done it! He had managed to control his temper. Now he was the master. Now he could determine how the rest of the conversation would go.

"It is too bad that I cannot tell you of Cotauna's wishes," O-Tah-Wah sighed, "but then, my instructions were very clear, and you are most certainly not the priest who is to be told of these secret things."

For once, it was not O-Tah-Wah who was furious. Eagle Wing *was*, however. "If you know of something that would affect Cotauna's funeral, speak!" His words came in a loud, hissing whisper. The priest could hardly stand this. Here was an opportunity for him to advance his station in the tribe, and yet he could not get this limping fool to tell him the secret!

Carefully, O-Tah-Wah watched the changing expressions on the young face. He knew that it would take great skill now if he was to achieve his purpose. Still, O-Tah-Wah knew that he had nothing to lose. Better to try and fail than to simply let the Flatheads kill him in the stupid notion that his spirit could serve Cotauna for eternity. With these thoughts in mind, O-Tah-Wah set the next step of his plan in motion.

"I have been thinking," he began carefully, "that it has been you alone who has shown an interest in me. You have even brought me food. While it is plain that you are not the one of whom Cotauna spoke, why should you not have the honor rather than one of the other priests? After all, they have done nothing for me." O-Tah-Wah then appeared to be thinking very hard. He frowned and wrinkled his brow. He blinked his eyes and rubbed his chin. It was quite a performance!

Eagle Wing swallowed his anger and tried to smile. Once more, he appeared to work at the decorating, but he was only pretending. Close to the slave's ear, he whispered quickly, "You are right, my friend." The priest was smiling broadly by now; there was still a chance that this idiot might tell him something which he could use in his struggle to take Cotauna's place as the leader of the Mound Builders.

"I do not want to tell you of these secret matters here, where the others might hear," O-Tah-Wah said, looking puzzled. "Where shall we be kept this night?"

"You and the others will be left here in the temple under guard if the purifying of your bodies is completed. If not, you must return to the slave's stockade."

"You must see to it that the purifying is not completed," O-Tah-Wah told him, "so that we shall be taken back to the prison. Late tonight, when the evening star is halfway up the sky, you will come to the stockade. Then, if you have brought the proper things with you, Cotauna's secret will be yours. Of course, you will have to arrange to have our guard dismissed. It would not do for him to hear."

Eagle Wing was immediately suspicious. "All of this can easily be done," he began, "but what are these 'things' that you are asking me to bring?"

"I want a war bow and a full quiver of arrows. Also, a spear-thrower and many darts to use with it!"

The priest stared at him in shocked disbelief. "Why do you

ask this?" he gasped. "Surely you know that it is death to anyone who gives weapons to a slave."

"I know that it is death to him who is *caught*," O-Tah-Wah replied calmly. "That is why you must be very careful."

"But what do you plan to do with these things?" The priest's tone was almost one of admiration. Never had he met such a person as O-Tah-Wah.

"I plan to escape!" O-Tah-Wah spat the words boldly into the face of the greedy young priest.

Several of the other priests were watching the two men closely. Both O-Tah-Wah and Eagle Wing became aware of it at nearly the same moment. This ended their planning. The crippled slave felt now, however, that there was a good chance the priest might respond to the plan. Greed and ambition make fine bait for any kind of a trap.

Eagle Wing was thinking carefully. The guard would be no problem. He could simply tell the warrior on duty that certain rites must be done to those slaves chosen to die. He could get the weapons easily, too. As far as the escape itself was concerned, it made no difference to him. He was sure that no slave could get away from the Mound Builders anyway. Many had tried, but he could remember very few who had succeeded. What did he have to lose? Suppose the young fool actually did try to run. He would be promptly caught and put to death. Eagle Wing felt more and more sure that he should meet the slave at the appointed hour.

The stone cup that Eagle Wing had been using struck the baked clay floor and splashed red ochre paint across the legs of the two nearest slaves. The other priests grumbled at the carelessness of their brother Eagle Wing. Now they would have to take the chosen ones back to the stockade for the night. The purifying rites would have to be finished on the following day. Eagle Wing looked very sorry about the "accident" he had caused. As the guards marched the slaves out of the temple, a quick look passed between Eagle Wing and O-Tah-Wah. The bargain was made.

Unlike the dazed feeling he'd had on the way to the temple, O-Tah-Wah's mind now was sharp and clear. He felt sure that the weapons would be brought. If nothing else, the fugitives would now have a chance to defend themselves when the Flatheads chased them.

Only one problem seemed to remain. O-Tah-Wah was thinking hard about it as they trudged along. The problem was food. With the crude weapons they had made, and the very fine ones that Eagle Wing was to supply, the fugitives might be able to kill enough animals to stay alive, even during this month when game was scarce. O-Tah-Wah knew, however, that they would have no time for hunting! It would be a lucky thing if they could escape at all. And if they did make their way to freedom, it would be by constant travel. No, there would be no hunting once they made their break. They must have food that could be carried along—something light, but filling and nourishing. O-Tah-Wah still had not thought of a solution as he reached the ugly little jail. "Perhaps," he thought happily, "my good friend Bruin will have the answer." Thinking of Bruin made him feel better than he had for some time. O-Tah-Wah had feared he would never again see the huge, kindly man.

The fire was burning brightly inside the stockade. The slaves who had not been chosen were sitting around it, too tense for sleep. They were mourning their friends whom they imagined already dead. The astonishment on their faces was almost humorous as all five of their comrades were pushed into the room. Bruin leaped up and grabbed O-Tah-Wah in a crushing bear hug befitting his name. O-Tah-Wah yowled in pain as the giant's arms continued to squeeze his thin body.

"What do you have to tell us? What is it that has happened?" they asked all together. "We thought that by now your spirits would be busy serving the ghost of Cotauna! How did you manage to return here?"

O-Tah-Wah told them all that had taken place. He left the story of his bargain with Eagle Wing for last. When they heard of it, the others were delighted with the trick. Bruin, however, was very quiet. There was great danger in any plan that involved one of the priests. Bruin knew them to be arrogant, cruel men, but he was also well aware that they were not foolish. The giant did not enter further into the happy talk. He must think and plan well before the appointed time.

It was good that Bruin, at least, was thinking, for Eagle Wing was making careful preparations, too. The little surprise he was planning for the chosen slaves was designed to make their escape somewhat more difficult!

CHAPTER 10

The Fugitives' Flight

The stockade fire was burning much brighter than usual. Bruin and O-Tah-Wah had decided that this would give them a slight advantage when Eagle Wing arrived. His eyes would be used to the darkness, and the bright firelight inside the stockade would make him blink for a moment or two. If the plan worked as Bruin and O-Tah-Wah hoped it would, a few minutes would be all that were needed.

O-Tah-Wah paced nervously around the stockade. He checked the skin bedrolls to be sure they looked as realistic as possible. Each slave attempting the escape had filled his bedroll with husks and dirt. The slaves then hid themselves in the room on each side of the door. When Eagle Wing entered, they planned to overpower him, as well as any guards who might be with him. The crude weapons prepared by O-Tah-Wah and Bruin made them feel brave and strong. The thought of getting more weapons provided even greater excitement. All but Bruin felt sure of success.

The eight men who were to try for the escape were completely dressed. They had tied skins around their feet and legs, for the Flatheads had taken away the new moccasins the priests had given them. It was yet another clever method of discouraging runaways.

The roaring fire made the stockade too warm for the fully dressed men, but it was nearly time for Eagle Wing to arrive. The slaves did not want to waste a second when he came. There would be no time to put on more clothing then, so they stood against the log walls as far from the fire as possible, and sweated.

Every man was armed in some way, although some of their "weapons" were merely wooden clubs or sharpened, fire-hardened sticks. Bruin looked at the position each man had taken. He moved two of them a little, then began speaking in a loud whisper. "You must remember that according to the plan we have all agreed upon, we shall leave the village together. Once beyond the new mound, we shall break up by two's. Each pair of men will leave the group at a different place, until only O-Tah-Wah and I are still traveling north. Once alone, each pair will be on its own. There will be no attempt to regroup. This would be foolish and dangerous. May the Great Spirit help us all!"

"Do not forget," O-Tah-Wah joined in, "that we must take the time to break into the storehouse and fill our pouches with ground corn. Let no one fail to do this, for without food, we will soon tire and then most certainly be caught."

The problem of food had been solved by one of the older slaves who was too sick to go with the escapees. He had made little comment on the preparations, but his excellent suggestion about food had been taken immediately. He had suggested that ground corn could be eaten on the run; it was light in weight and would provide a nourishing meal. The extra time needed to get the food would be very dangerous, but there was absolutely no way to avoid the risk. The most they could do was to hope that the storehouse would not be guarded on this raw and windy night.

All whispering finally stopped. The slaves stood pressed against the inside walls on each side of the door. They stared straight ahead, heat and nervousness soaking them with perspiration.

Bruin was troubled. He had stationed himself to the left of the door, for he was to grab Eagle Wing as he entered. Wrestling with the Flathead was not the problem on his mind, however. The giant was worried about the three slaves who were not going. One was too old and he would only slow the others down. Bruin watched the old man for several moments. There was little doubt as to what would become of him. After the escape, it would be these slaves left behind who must die at the funeral of Cotauna!

The other two slaves who would remain behind were ill. One of them was barely conscious, while the other was in pain almost all of the time. Bruin thought hard. He did not wish to see anyone left behind to suffer and die. The giant's big ugly face was wrinkled with thought and worry. There was to be no time for a plan, however, for at that moment they all heard the sound of footsteps crunching through the crusted snow. The sound was plain, even above the crackle of the flames. Certain that Eagle Wing was approaching, the slaves stood motionless. Even their breathing stopped as they listened.

For a moment, all was silent. Then the footsteps could be heard again, moving closer. A few words drifted softly through the log walls, but they were too faint to be understood. O-Tah-Wah's heart was hammering wildly as he held his breath and listened. Bruin's eyes were bulging with excitement and fright. The other men stared straight ahead, muscles tensed and trembling.

The heavy log door began to move. As the slaves flattened themselves even tighter against the walls, they stared expectantly at the door. Once the door was opened wide enough to admit a man, it stopped moving. Then there was silence. The waiting was so unbearable that the slaves were about to burst with anxiety. But still Eagle Wing did not enter. A full minute passed without a sound. Suddenly, O-Tah-Wah heard his name whispered urgently from outside. Bruin heard it, too, and instantly he realized their mistake. Eagle Wing was too sly to enter the stockade. Instead, he wanted O-Tah-Wah to come out. "Without a doubt," Bruin thought, "Eagle Wing has other warriors hidden nearby!" The giant was near panic. If O-Tah-Wah left the stockade now, they might never see each other again. Frozen by fear and indecision, no one moved. O-Tah-Wah's name was called again, more loudly this time.

Bruin, the one who was always in control, the one who kept himself calm, now lost his head completely! With a bellow he leaped to the door and smashed it wide open. He charged courageously into the night, swinging his club widely. O-Tah-Wah and the others bounded after the fierce giant, screaming and yelling like crazy men. Their makeshift weapons were ready, but there was nothing for them to hit! The bright firelight inside the stockade made the charging slaves virtually blind in the blackness beyond the door. The very advantage they had counted on had worked against them.

Eagle Wing had indeed brought warriors with him. As a priest of the Mound Builders, this was his right and privilege. These 10 warriors now closed in quickly from their hiding places. Eagle Wing watched from a safe place. His eyes, accustomed to the darkness, quite easily took in the confused scene before him. The moon on the patchy snow, coupled with the light streaming through the open doorway, provided quite enough light for him and his warriors.

Eagle Wing's warriors attacked with speed and power. Bruin went down first, struck by a Mound Builder war club. The weapon was a leather-covered stone ball attached to a short thick handle. O-Tah-Wah took a blow on the shoulder—a blow so powerful that it would have crushed his skull. Furious, the crippled slave lashed out blindly with the butt end of his crude spear. The weapon found a target and one of the guards snarled in pain.

Bruin lumbered to his feet, gasping and choking as he tried to fill his empty lungs with air. The guard who had struck him stood stupidly, gaping at the size of the man he had felled. The giant, however, was now up again. But the Flathead raised his club too late for another blow. Bruin's hand shot out like a striking snake, ripping the club from the enemy's grasp before he realized what was happening. Bruin would have brained his tormentor immediately, but the man dashed away into the darkness.

O-Tah-Wah was in the midst of the fight, jabbing and striking with his spear. It was so dark that most of the time he could not even be sure it was the enemy he was fighting. The Mound Builders, however, were even more confused. The priests, in dressing the chosen slaves for the coming sacrifice, had made them look exactly like themselves. In the darkness, it was most difficult for the Flatheads to know whom to hit.

Bruin was almost completely recovered now, and he battled his way to O-Tah-Wah's side, knocking the Mound Builders out of his way as he came. Three of the Flatheads, badly wounded or unconscious, were out of the fray, and the others were weakening fast. They had not counted on the desperate fight the slaves were putting up. Fighting his way to his friend's side, Bruin knocked another Flathead down with a sidewise flip of the club he had "borrowed." O-Tah-Wah, glad to see his friend approaching through the darkness, took new courage. With a savage lunge he seized the arms of a warrior just drawing his bow. He wrestled the man to the ground, then clubbed him twice with the thick shaft of his spear.

Eagle Wing, alarmed at the way the battle was going, now decided to step into the fight himself. He ran quickly toward the scuffling men. Before he had even reached the edge of the fray, one of the slaves knocked him to his knees with a hickory club. Eagle Wing had never been hurt before, and the experience was horrible. He gave up immediately, cowering back against the stockade door in terror.

The remaining guards, seeing the priest's example, stopped fighting, too, and quite suddenly it was over.

Bruin took charge. The victors pushed the dazed and bleeding Mound Builders into the stockade. Eagle Wing, whimpering like a whipped puppy, was shoved inside, too. O-Tah-Wah and two of the others rushed madly about, dragging the wounded Flatheads into the stockade. Time was of the greatest importance. Every moment that passed lessened their chances of leaving the village undetected.

Eagle Wing had brought the promised weapons, although it was now plain that he'd had no intention of actually keeping his end of the bargain. Eagle Wing had thought that when O-Tah-Wah saw the weapons, he would reveal Cotauna's secret. As soon as the information had been given, Eagle Wing had planned to summon the hidden warriors. They would simply throw O-Tah-Wah back into the stockade and guard it well till morning. It was a good plan, but Eagle Wing had made a serious mistake: he had not considered how badly *each one* of the chosen slaves wanted to stay alive!

With the clubs, bows, and axes of the warriors, plus the beautiful weapons brought by Eagle Wing, the captives were so well armed they felt that no one could stop them. All but Bruin and O-Tah-Wah were hurrying anxiously around, preparing to leave immediately. One of the slaves, seeing Eagle Wing on his knees in the filthy husks, raised a war club to strike. O-Tah-Wah's senses were still wild from the battle, and he watched with a bitter smile as the priest sobbed and pleaded for his life. Just in time, Bruin stepped in and grabbed the slave's wrist.

"There will be no killing!" he growled savagely. "We shall not lower ourselves by murdering our captives. This is exactly what the Flatheads do. We are not like them. There will be no killing!" The giant stood there, still holding the slave's arm. No one argued with Bruin!

"Very well," O-Tah-Wah snapped, "we let them live, but now we must go. Some of the warriors probably escaped. They will waken the entire village before long."

"Do we have time to raid the corn bin?" one of the slaves asked anxiously. They were all wild to run into the forest and keep going. Their only thought was to get as far away from these people as possible.

"No," O-Tah-Wah answered, "we do not have time to get the food. We must kill what we need as we travel. Now let us go!"

"We go," Bruin stated flatly "to the grain shed and fill the pouches we have made. We shall do this just as we planned. Any of you who tries to leave the village before the grain has been taken must deal first with me!"

"The rest of you may go where you please," one slave stated, his lips curled in a sneer. "I am leaving now, this moment, and

I have no intention of going anywhere *near* the corn hut!" His words had hardly been uttered before Bruin moved. A loud crack was plainly heard as the huge open hand glanced off the side of the outspoken slave's head. Knocked completely off his feet, the slave nearly fell into the fire. Bruin kicked him back from the flames' reach and then turned and looked at each of his companions. No one else decided to leave!

"To the corn bin, then!" O-Tah-Wah shouted. They rushed into the cold night, carrying their weapons at the ready. Only a few minutes were required to close the door and drop the heavy log bar into place across it. They would not have to worry about the Flatheads in the stockade, but Bruin had seen at least one of the Flatheads run from the battle.

The fugitives raced through the trees toward the southwest corner of the village where the ground corn was kept. It was pitch black under the trees. Had they not known the area so well, it is doubtful that they could have found their way through the grove. No attention was paid to branches that whipped their faces and tore at their clothes. Whenever they fell, which was often, they could only scramble to their feet and run again.

By the time they finally broke out of the trees, O-Tah-Wah had dropped several hundred feet behind. The Lazy One had caught on every branch and root it passed. Angrily, O-Tah-Wah dragged the stiff limb along, well aware that he was holding the other men back. They had stopped now to wait for him. O-Tah-Wah was sure that Bruin had made the others wait until he was able to catch up. At last, O-Tah-Wah crashed out of the bushes and joined the others. They were huddled together and whispering rapidly.

Bruin put one arm over the shoulders of his small friend. "We each take as much ground corn as the pouches will hold," he told O-Tah-Wah hurriedly. "The storage building is just across this clearing. We must do all we can to avoid being seen. Should the guards find us now, they will be on our tracks with morning's first light. If we can leave without being discovered, it may take some time before they find our tracks. We need all the time we can get!"

The giant sent two smaller slaves scurrying across the clearing. These men were to scout the storage shed. If it was not guarded, they would whistle for the others to follow. The waiting was terrible, but after what seemed like hours, a low whistle floated across the moonlit clearing. Swiftly, the other slaves darted across the silvery snow patches toward the small rounded bin that held the village's winter corn rations.

O-Tah-Wah could well remember the first time he had seen this building. The young hunter had marvelled at the idea of food stored in one place where the whole village could get it as needed. In his own village, people had always feared the long winter because of the hunger it often brought. When the hunting was bad, or the acorns were not plentiful, winter had meant the ache of an empty stomach. Babies and children would cry, and their mothers would look very sad. Even tonight, as he was attempting escape, O-Tah-Wah could not help admiring the cleverness of the Mound Builders. But his admiration of them did not lessen his desire for freedom.

The slaves had no trouble entering the building. The baskets of corn were not what the slaves were after. Bruin climbed up on some of the baskets and reached toward the roof, where the small skin bags of ground corn were hanging. This mixture was ready to eat as it was. The giant ripped the bags from their leather thongs and threw several of them to his companions. They did not try to divide the food in the darkness of the shed but hurried outside. Bruin insisted that the door be closed just as they had found it. If the slaves left any sign that they had been here, the Flatheads would very quickly put the dogs on their trail.

O-Tah-Wah, being the most familiar with the land north of the village, led the little band at a fast trot. It was still very hard to see, even in the clearing. The moonlight on the melting snow, however, made enough light for them. There were many tracks in the snow near the village, so they did not need to avoid the snowy patches.

O-Tah-Wah took them in a great circle to the west, hoping to miss the main part of the village entirely before heading north again. Occasionally, they were confused in their directions, but looking at the position of the stars soon set them right. When they slipped down the bank of a small stream, O-Tah-Wah knew they had traveled far enough to the west. They crossed noisily, the thin ice digging into their shins as it broke with every step. O-Tah-Wah struggled up the far bank, the Lazy One already turning numb with cold. As soon as they were clear of the thick brush that lined the creek bank, O-Tah-Wah turned north, leading the shivering men in a fast jog. Slowly, the chill worked its way out of their legs as they ran.

O-Tah-Wah liked to be the leader. For one thing, he had never had this sort of companionship before. As a child playing with the other boys in his village, his stiff leg had always left him far behind. By running first, he could set a pace that the Lazy One could keep up fairly well. Several times he tripped, but the others fell occasionally, too, so no one noticed.

The faint light of dawn finally began to light the way. The village was behind the fugitives now, but they were still far from being out of danger.

The runaway slaves slowed to a fast walk. O-Tah-Wah chose the route heading straight toward the North Star, which was still faintly visible in the rapidly lightening sky. Suddenly he stopped, raising a war axe high to signal the others, who followed single file behind him. The sound O-Tah-Wah thought he had heard did not come again, so he started to move once more. There! This time they all heard it. Terror struck them to stone as they listened. Faintly, the yelping of several dogs could be heard far behind them. Dogs were what each of them feared most. A man tracking his prey could often be fooled by various tricks. But a dog, if it was a good tracker, could never be misled for long.

It was now time for the slaves to go their separate ways. Capture was almost certain for those slaves the dogs chose to track. All of them had known this before they left, however, so each pair of slaves was ready to take its chance alone.

O-Tah-Wah and Bruin gripped the hands of each slave in turn, then trotted off, still heading straight north. By doing so, they were putting themselves in the greatest danger of all, for the dogs would probably continue to follow the straight trail, paying little attention to those that led away to the east and west.

It was light now, although the sun had not yet risen above the horizon. Birds were chirping in the treetops, and as usual in Mound Builder hunting grounds, they fluttered rapidly away at the sight of men.

O-Tah-Wah thought of the morning, much like this one, when he had first realized he was within the territory of the Flatheads. Angrily, he recalled the treatment they had given him, and the slavery he had been forced to accept. "I *must* escape! I *must* escape! I *must* escape!" he thought over and over again.

Quite suddenly, O-Tah-Wah and Bruin both heard the dogs again. There was no doubt that the barking was closer now. O-Tah-Wah stopped to listen, his chest heaving as the breath burst from his nose and mouth in explosive clouds of steam.

Bruin, too, was panting hard. Both slaves, although strong and well, were not used to this kind of running. O-Tah-Wah could remember the time when he could have kept up a strenuous pace of walking and running for many hours. But now, many miles were yet before them, and behind were the Mound Builders and their dogs.

Bruin spoke between breaths as they walked on. "We must now find a stream, Little Brother. Perhaps you know of a river or creek near here that you crossed at the time of your capture?"

"Yes," O-Tah-Wah answered as they started to run again, "I believe there is a small creek." The crippled hunter knew that running water was their only hope of getting the dogs off their trail. But the stream he remembered meandered through the rolling hills like a curving crawling snake. What they needed was a large stream, one swift enough to have open water at the center, and one that followed a reasonably straight course. O-Tah-Wah could remember no such stream anywhere near their present location.

The deep baying of the vicious tracking dogs sounded again. It was even clearer this time. O-Tah-Wah's heart sank as he realized that the sound still came from directly behind them. The dogs had not noticed the trails of the other pairs of slaves leading away to the east and west. The dogs and the Flatheads were following straight north. Each minute brought them closer and closer to the running giant and his crippled friend.

As he slid and half-fell down a steep bank, O-Tah-Wah wondered if the lead dog was one of those trained to kill. He scrambled to the bottom of the little valley and started up the other slope. He was not sorry they had made the attempt, even though it now looked as if their careful plans had been made for nothing.

As they crested still another of the softly rolling hills, Bruin, who was now leading, shouted for joy. Below them and slightly to the east, a silvery ribbon of broad water could be seen twisting its way in a curving but northerly direction. It was the river—their road to freedom. Bruin and O-Tah-Wah pounded each other on the back and laughed with delight. Gasping and panting in the cold air, both slaves were so happy they almost forgot the grim, determined Mound Builders who were moving rapidly on their trail.

The animals had been silent for some time, but at this moment, their barking suddenly began again. It was so much louder this time that the slaves jumped at the sound. Their laughter stopped very quickly, for the river was at least a mile away.

New hope gave them added strength. Without taking time to talk, they both set the fastest pace possible. There was no reason to hold back now. They must reach the river before the lead dog caught up to them. Once in the stream, they could slow down, for the dogs would not be able to track them at all after they entered the water.

Bruin pulled rapidly ahead, his long legs and powerful body quickly outdistancing his limping companion.

"Wait!" O-Tah-Wah hated to call out, but Bruin was nearly out of sight. He was suddenly afraid of becoming separated from his friend. Bruin slowed to a trot, looking back sheepishly as O-Tah-Wah struggled gamely across the bushes and brush between them.

Suddenly, Bruin stiffened, staring intently up at the ridge they had just left. He had seen a flash of moving brown flitting across a small opening in the trees.

"Go on! Go on!" the giant urged as O-Tah-Wah caught up to him at last. "Until we reach the river, you must go first." O-Tah-

Wah nodded and trotted ahead, puzzled by the way Bruin kept watching their back trail.

They ran on, but this time it was Bruin who fell behind. Throwing a quick look over his shoulder, O-Tah-Wah was surprised to see that the big slave had not only dropped even farther back, but had drawn the Mound Builder war club from his belt!

O-Tah-Wah, who had never had a friend before, and who had once doubted even Bruin's friendship, was about to learn the real meaning of the word!

CHAPTER 11

Kandao

The huge black-and-brown beast was no longer trotting with his muzzle near the earth. Now he traveled at a fast lope. The trail was so fresh that his keen hunter's nose could pick the human scent out of the air itself. Had the dog known where to look, he would have been able to see the men he was tracking. They were running not far ahead of him, toward the bank of the river.

The dripping tongue flopped this way and that as the winded animal galloped along. The wolf blood that flowed in his veins drove the dog onward. He had but one goal—to overtake and attack those who ran before him.

The rest of the pack was far behind by now. The other dogs, confused by the trails of those slaves who had changed direction, had been severely beaten by the angry Flatheads. In their anger at the delay, the Flatheads had kicked and whipped the dogs until the animals had run off, howling, into the woods. Much time was lost before they could be rounded up and set back on the trail. Little Eyes, who was in charge of the search party, was furious.

"Kandao," as he was called by the Mound Builders, was the only dog that had not been confused. He had run straight on, following the same trail he had first been shown at the corn shed. This dog was the most vicious and cunning animal the Flatheads owned. Even his own keepers feared and hated the cruel pack leader. *Kandao* meant "smiling one." The name fit well, for the shaggy beast could rarely be seen when his lips were not drawn back, showing his fangs in an ugly snarl.

The dog suddenly slowed his fast pace to a stiff-legged walk, then stopped entirely. The ribs showed plainly under his matted fur as he stood motionless in a patch of shade. The killer had caught sight of his enemy.

The dog's eyes were all that moved as he watched the running man ahead of him. Even Kandao's heavy breathing was stilled. The killer noted the slave's speed and direction carefully. All this was done by instinct, for it was part of the stalk. Kandao was preparing to attack!

The dog began to move at last. His first steps were quick and graceful. In a half-crouch, he ran swiftly to the next cover. The large, slightly slanted eyes never strayed for a moment from the running slave ahead of him. Another skulking, silent dash brought the killer dog even closer. He stopped then, once again as still and motionless as an animal carved of wood.

The dog did not know if the running men had seen him or not. This would have made no difference anyway. Thousands of years of animal instinct were demanding that Kandao act in this way. The stalk, once begun, could end in only one way—attack, followed by fighting and death. The time had come.

O-Tah-Wah, still ahead, had caught sight of the river gleaming through the trees before him. Bruin turned for a last look behind. He felt that by now it was safe to catch up to his friend at the riverbank. What he saw changed his plans, however. A big, mottled brown dog was bounding straight toward him!

Bruin recognized the animal immediately. He had guessed it was Kandao from the moment he had first caught a glimpse of the dog high on the ridge. The giant knew of at least three runaways the dog had killed over the past several years. "This time," the slave thought to himself as he turned to face the attack, "you will not be dragging down a starving, unarmed man already half-dead from running!"

O-Tah-Wah stopped for a moment and waited for Bruin to join him. Looking back for his friend, he was horrified at what he saw.

Snarling in fury, Kandao covered the last few yards in a series of stunning bounds. From six feet, he launched his powerful body straight at Bruin. Bruin could hear the rasping snarl as the "Smiling One" bared his gleaming fangs, hoping to sink them into his enemy's flesh. The animal's eyes were glazed with a blood lust that had gripped it the moment it had seen the runner.

Bruin, though badly winded, was ready for the charge. Kandao's heavy body struck him in the chest, just as the dog had intended. This man, however, did not fall down. The dog's jaws snapped shut on the handle of a war club instead of a soft throat. Before the dog could let go, Bruin smashed the killer's head with his left fist. The dog, snarling and growling, next tried for one of Bruin's legs. This time the stone ball on the end of the weapon struck him a crushing blow in the ribs. Stunned, the animal backed off a few steps. His pointed ears lay flattened against his head, and the fur along his neck and back stood out, stiff and thick. Again Kandao leaped, trying for the arm that held the club. This time the attack was launched with such fury that Bruin could not dodge in time. He felt sharp pain as the fangs slashed into his forearm and the powerful jaws closed in a crushing grip. The war club fell from his fingers. Trying to shake the animal loose, Bruin slipped and fell. Man and beast rolled over and over, the shouts and growls raising a horrible racket.

O-Tah-Wah, finally making a move, now ran straight into the fight. His spear was ready, but he could not use it for fear of hitting his friend. Suddenly, the dog released his hold on the arm. Once again, he lunged at Bruin's throat. As the dog leaped on top of the fallen slave, O-Tah-Wah saw the chance he had been waiting for. One short hard jab was all that was needed. The razor-sharp flint spearhead lanced into Kandao's shoulders. O-Tah-Wah yanked back on the shaft and prepared to strike again. But before he could do so, the bleeding animal leaped awkwardly sidewise, out of range. Without so much as a backward look Kandao limped away, whining in pain. The fight was over.

O-Tah-Wah helped Bruin to his feet. Without talking they both turned and raced for the river. The Mound Builders could not be far behind now.

Bruin was glad that his wound was not serious although his arm ached from the force of the dog's jaws.

They scrambled down a low hill to the river that lay broad and bright before them. Rushing to the water, they walked right in, breaking the thin ice near the shore with every step. The water was over their knees before they reached the center, where the current was stronger. Here there was no ice to show the direction they had taken.

The going was hard. Small stones on the bottom were slippery and some were sharp, as well. The water dragged at their legs, even though they tried to take high steps. Of course, the

Lazy One made walking in the river a nightmare. O-Tah-Wah's left leg could take a normal step, but then the stiff right limb would have to be dragged through the icy water all the way to the front again. The current was not great, but it, too, was against them.

Bruin tried to help his friend, but O-Tah-Wah shook him off angrily. The giant glanced at the smaller man. They had traveled less than three miles upstream, and already O-Tah-Wah could hardly keep up, even at the very slow pace they had set. The situation was serious. The slaves were just not making enough distance. Bruin thought hard. The dogs would not be able to track them in the stream, but the Flatheads would certainly follow along the banks for many miles, searching for the spot where the fugitives would leave the water.

As they rounded a sweeping bend in the river, a plan presented itself at last. A small creek, less than eight feet wide, flowed into the stream they had been following. Bruin strode ahead, the current pushing against his bulging thighs with every step. He headed straight into the creek's mouth.

"Where . . . are . . . you . . . going?" O-Tah-Wah had to gasp the question between great breaths. His wind was nearly gone.

"We have traveled far enough in the river," Bruin answered, still moving up the shallow creek. "Now we must try to outwit those who follow. My plan is to travel this creek to the west until we find a good place to leave the water. Then we must head northward once more."

O-Tah-Wah was grateful for any plan that would take them out of the deeper water. The current seemed to pull at his very flesh with every step. The pounding in his head was louder than war drums, and his lungs felt like fire. He was well aware that this sort of traveling would leave him totally exhausted within a few more hours.

The shallow water was hardly a problem for them compared to the way it had been in the river. And the little creek was also good for their plan. The current was swift enough to keep the water free of ice, and it was almost completely hidden under a thick growth of giant oaks and elms, now leafless and bare. The rivulet, however, was rapidly getting narrower. Soon there was hardly enough open water for them to walk in. They both knew that before long, they must leave the creek entirely.

This time, it was O-Tah-Wah who devised a trick to confuse the men seeking their trail. Noticing the thick branches that often hung low over the trail, he suddenly remembered the antics of a red fox he had once trailed as a boy. The clever little animal, finding itself forced to travel after a three-inch snow-fall, had outsmarted its young pursuer by leaping upon a fallen log that was partly clear of snow. Running to the far end of the log, the creature had then made a mighty bound, landing in a brushy thicket nearby. By the time O-Tah-Wah had figured out what had happened, the trail was cold, and the fox far away. O-Tah-Wah smiled as he remembered the incident. The two men stopped for a few precious moments, glad for a chance to catch their breath. O-Tah-Wah explained his plan quickly, and Bruin nodded. It was a good idea.

Both men began watching the trees now. Before long, they saw a large limb only a foot above their heads. The limb led to a massive trunk several yards beyond the creek bank. O-Tah-Wah leaped up, grabbing the bough with both hands. He swung his body back and forth a few times, then hoisted himself up onto the bough. In a few seconds he was sitting proudly on the limb, one leg hanging down from each side. He grinned widely at Bruin. It was true that his right leg was not as strong as it should be, but there was nothing wrong with either of his arms!

Bruin had more trouble. He was very strong but also very

heavy. O-Tah-Wah laughed aloud and taunted his friend as Bruin swung back and forth on the bough. Then Bruin began to laugh, too. Once he started laughing, it was impossible for the giant to boost himself up. They wasted too much time but somehow were too tired to care. "How wonderful it is," O-Tah-Wah thought happily, "how very wonderful, in time of great trouble, to have a friend!"

When both were finally mounted on the trembling oak limb, they inched their way along to the thick trunk. By climbing a few feet higher, they reached another branch. Following it allowed them to move another 20 feet away from the stream. Here they dropped to the ground. With good luck, the dogs might miss their trail entirely during their first two or three passes up and down the creek bank.

Neither man expected for a moment that these schemes would fool their enemy for long. The Flatheads would never give up as long as the runaways were still within their hunting grounds. Any trick that would confuse the Flatheads for even a short while, however, gave the slaves more time to keep moving north. North was the magic direction, for it was the nearest way out of the Flathead's territory. North meant safety. North meant home. North meant freedom!

The sun was more than halfway through its daily journey by now, so after traveling a fast two miles, Bruin called for a halt. He knew they must be careful not to exhaust themselves completely. Their flight would continue all through the coming night.

A ledge of rock jutting out of a steep bank provided a good shelter for the runaways. Bruin drew a leather pouch from its resting place against his chest. In it were two lumps of flint and a small supply of tinder. The giant fluffed up some of the soft, wool-like material and began striking the smaller flint block against the larger one. Anxiously, he clicked the corners together with short sharp blows. Sparks flew from the brittle stones, but the tinder refused to catch.

O-Tah-Wah paced about nervously, munching on a handful of ground corn from his small supply. He had already gathered enough dry wood for their fire, and with nothing to do, the young hunter became more and more nervous. "You will not be able to get the fire going," he finally told Bruin. "I believe it is taking too long. Let us run again now before the Flatheads find our trail!" He had hardly finished speaking when he noticed a thin spiral of smoke rising from between Bruin's hands. An ugly, crooked grin was Bruin's only reply.

Bruin blew gently on the smoldering tinder. The smoke grew thicker, and at last a small flame ate its way upward through the soft fibers. In a few moments, a hot fire was burning brightly among the round stones near their feet. O-Tah-Wah was amazed at the way the heat brought back his strength. The numbness in his legs and feet was slowly replaced by a tingling, prickly feeling, as if a thousand sharp thorns were being gently touched against every part of his skin. The Lazy One stopped aching, too. O-Tah-Wah could now see the necessity for the fire.

Bruin knew that an escaping slave's greatest desire was to run on and on until he dropped from exhaustion. There would be no better way to be recaptured. Both Bruin and O-Tah-Wah had discussed this in their long whispered conversations back in the stockade. Had it been left up to O-Tah-Wah, however, they would have made this very mistake.

Bruin and O-Tah-Wah munched their cornmeal, all the time turning their bodies this way and that, letting the welcome heat soak into every muscle. Steam rose from wet buckskin, its musky odor reminding them both of more pleasant times and happier days.

The minutes passed quickly, and too soon it was time to move on again. Bruin covered the fire with several handfuls of dry earth taken from a sheltered place under the rock ledge. O-Tah-Wah finished the job by scattering a few sticks and leaves over the spot to hide it from those who might follow.

The skins they wore were still far from dry, but both men were used to wet clothes. As slaves, they had been wet most of the time.

The fire and food gave them new strength, and just as important, new spirit and a desire to win their race for freedom. They trotted in single file, O-Tah-Wah leading the way. Slanting, golden rays flashed through the forest glades as the afternoon sun dropped steadily toward the forest on their left. The light would soon be gone. Neither slave allowed himself to think of what was coming with the darkness. Traveling this hilly, brushy country at night was frightening, even to think about.

When they could jog no longer, they walked. Even then the pace was fast, and the miles slipped steadily by, each one taking them closer to the Mound Builders' northern boundry. The hills were still steep, but it seemed that they were somewhat smaller now.

Just before darkness closed in, they had a fine piece of luck. A running stream nearly free of ice and quite shallow appeared before them. Its rippling, silvery surface shining pearl-white in the twilight appeared to O-Tah-Wah as the very road to freedom. Bruin, however, had other ideas.

"Here we shall trick the Flatheads again!" he crowed, peering up and down the stream.

"What do you mean?"

"This river," the giant replied quickly, "runs almost directly north and south. The Flatheads will expect us to enter it and continue toward the "Star Which Never Moves."

"But we *should* head north!" cried O-Tah-Wah. Panic showed on his face as he tried to see his friend's expression in the darkness. What could Bruin be planning?

"You are very tired," the giant explained, "much more walking in the cold river will certainly cause you to become lame tomorrow. Besides, you are a fine hunter. Surely you know that the easiest animal to trail is the black bear. Is this not so?"

O-Tah-Wah's muscular shoulders were rising and falling mightily as he gulped in the cold night air. He stared wistfully northward. "Yes, it is so," he finally answered, wiping the cold sweat from his forehead.

"And you know *why* the black bear is so simple to follow, do you not?" It was too dark to tell if a grin accompanied Bruin's question, but the smaller man suspected one.

"Because it always does just what one would *expect* it to do," O-Tah-Wah replied disgustedly. He was already turning southward, feeling his way through the thick growth along the stream bank.

After a stumbling, groping mile, the giant told O-Tah-Wah to leap into the stream and cross to the far side. Once on the other bank, he was to head north again. Bruin would continue south for another mile, then he too would cross and try to catch up with his friend by midnight.

They had no way of knowing if their schemes were working. If successful, each trick would give the slaves a little more time to travel farther. Should the Mound Builders not be fooled, however, the hours used up in this way would only allow their pursuers to catch up more quickly.

They had no difficulty meeting again some two hours later, but Bruin was disappointed that O-Tah-Wah had not gone farther. There was no use fooling themselves any longer. They were both tired, but the smaller slave could hardly travel.

"We must stop and rest now," Bruin panted, pushing his way through a clump of chokeberry bushes. O-Tah-Wah grunted his agreement, and they started moving away from the stream to higher ground where they could make camp.

In the darkness, it was impossible to find wood for a fire, so the slaves huddled together under the low-hanging branches of a spruce tree. The night was not as cold as they had feared. At first they were very cold, but once the perspiration dried from their bodies, the shivering stopped and they finally managed to fall asleep.

Dawn found them awake and running again. But Bruin was very worried. They were traveling too slowly. He tried to keep his concern hidden from his friend, but O-Tah-Wah was also aware that their plans were not working out as well as they had hoped.

During their first rest stop, O-Tah-Wah spent several minutes massaging the muscles in the lower calf of his good leg. Bruin watched this with alarm but said nothing. As soon as they had caught their breath, they started off again at a fast walk. They hadn't traveled a mile when O-Tah-Wah began to groan. He gritted his teeth and kept going, but his breath whistled loudly in and out through clenched teeth. Bruin knew exactly what the trouble was. O-Tah-Wah had a muscle cramp.

"Stop," Bruin told his friend suddenly. "I can tell that your leg is hurting you. Let me see where the pain is." O-Tah-Wah sat down gingerly, the Lazy One sticking out at its usual angle. There was no need to tell the giant where the pain was. An angry lump was growing on the bulging muscle behind and slightly below the knee.

"It is no use," O-Tah-Wah sighed bitterly. "I have already slowed you down too much because of the Lazy One. Now with the other leg aching, too, I cannot go on. You go ahead. I shall rest here and catch up with you later." But neither man was fooled by this remark.

"Lie down on your stomach," Bruin ordered, paying no attention to O-Tah-Wah's urgings that he go on alone. "This will hurt," he said bluntly. O-Tah-Wah soon learned the truth of this last remark!

As O-Tah-Wah lay face-down on the cold ground, Bruin took his stolen war club in both hands. Without any apology, he began using the thick shaft like a rolling pin, crushing down across the knotted muscle. The pain was very bad, but O-Tah-Wah did not cry out. Back and forth the thick handle went rolling, smashing the kinks out of the overworked leg.

Getting to his feet, O-Tah-Wah was amazed at how relaxed the muscle felt. He took a few careful steps. His leg still hurt, but he could walk and even trot a little.

Feeling better now, O-Tah-Wah began to tell himself that their escape was assured. But Bruin, who had been a slave for many years, knew better!

CHAPTER 12

The Last Stand

Little Eyes was raging! He stomped angrily about, shouting orders and generally getting in the way. The chief was wondering if he had made a mistake in not sending messengers to nearby villages with news of the escape. Although he knew that this was usually done, Little Eyes was ashamed to have others know that the slaves had escaped. He also realized too late that the guards should have been doubled around the slave quarters at the time of Cotauna's death. But he had forgotten to do this. Also, Little Eyes had not thought that the priest Eagle Wing could have been so easily fooled by a mere slave. For his stupidity, Eagle Wing would die.

Three of the dogs had finally been caught and were being brought back to the main party. The frightened animals fought the leather leashes, twisting their heads about and stubbornly standing their ground. Their keepers yanked viciously on the rawhide, dragging the dogs farther and farther away from the trail they had been following. Had the men believed the half-starved animals, they would have captured two of the slaves in less than an hour. But Little Eyes was so sure that all the escapees would run straight north that he did not trust the dogs' tracking ability.

At that moment, a shout was raised from one of the Mound Builders who had been tracking on ahead. "Kandao! Kandao!" his voice boomed through the forest, summoning the rest of the men on the run.

Little Eyes smiled cruelly at the news. "I knew that Kandao, at least, would do the work," he told a companion. Both of them were hurrying up a long hill toward the man who had called. At the top they stood still, watching the wounded dog trying to climb the opposite slope. All of the Flatheads were amazed. They could see that the killer dog had been badly hurt. "Forward!" the chief roared, brandishing his short war spear. It was plain to him now that the enemy was indeed straight ahead of them to the north. They set off at a run, the three recaptured dogs leading the way. Kandao was ignored.

Bruin's plan had worked. The other slaves were safe for at least a day or two. If they kept traveling and luck was with them, their chances of escape were good.

The dogs the Flatheads were now forced to use were not good trackers. Without Kandao's leadership, they scattered like leaves in the wind. Time after time, they lost the trail completely. It was then necessary to drag the animals in ever-larger circles until the trail could be found again. Several times the Flatheads themselves discovered the trail by sight, long before the snuffling, skinny beasts had found the scent.

Darkness was almost upon them by the time the Flatheads finally discovered how the two slaves had left the larger stream without leaving a trail. Little Eyes peered angrily into the gloomy glades along the little tributary. It was he who had guessed that this creek was the slaves' escape route. The chief gave a few orders, and soon the Flatheads were making a rough camp. They would be up at dawn to continue the chase.

* * * * *

Despite Bruin's frequent and vicious massages with the war club's handle, O-Tah-Wah's leg cramps kept returning. The giant tried everything he could think of to help, but their progress grew slower and slower.

As O-Tah-Wah felt still another clawing pain in the calf of his good leg, he let himself sink to the ground in despair. The moment his weight was off the limb, several muscles knotted painfully, drawing his foot upward in a crooked twist.

"It is useless to go farther now," Bruin announced. "We shall make camp here to give you time to rest and get warm. As soon as the leg will hold your weight, we must travel again."

O-Tah-Wah did not argue. What good would it have done? He knew quite well that Bruin was right. Bitterly, he stared at the ground. He was not even able to help his friend gather brush for the fire. "It is not *fair*!" he told himself fiercely. "All of my life I have wanted a friend. Now that I have found one, I am worse than useless to him." He paid no attention to the pains he felt in almost every part of his body. "If only I could be of some value to my friend," he thought in desperation.

The fire was burning brightly by this time. The crippled slave stared at the flames. His eyes were sad and troubled as he stretched both legs toward the heat.

Munching on a mouthful of cornmeal, Bruin watched his friend. No words were needed between them, for each was certain of the other's thoughts. "Do not worry, my brother," Bruin said, making his voice as cheerful as possible. "We are far, far ahead of the stupid Flatheads by now. There is no reason why we should not catch a few moments' rest. Besides, I am much too tired to take even one more step."

O-Tah-Wah turned and looked closely at the big man who squatted beside him. The lies were clumsy, and the small hunter believed not a word. He knew why Bruin had said these things, however, and thinking about it made a lump in his throat. He looked quickly away, turning his gaze back into the fire, for his eyes were filled with tears.

As the flames flickered and danced among the charred sticks, O-Tah-Wah found himself thinking the strangest of thoughts. "What does one do for such a friend?" he thought hopelessly. How could he know when he had never had a friend before? For some reason, he thought often of Turtle Shell and the story Bruin had told him.

At last he began allowing himself to form the thought that had been lurking around the edges of his mind for some time. "I owe Bruin a great deal," he thought. "If we continue running together, I can only slow him down more and more. Soon we shall both be captured. My duty is clear. I shall lay down my life so that my friend may be saved." The moment the idea took form in his brain, O-Tah-Wah was certain it was the right one. For the first time in many hours, he felt the pride of a man who has something to offer.

The young hunter squared his shoulders proudly and turned to Bruin. "My leg is much better now," he announced firmly. He was already rising to his feet. "Let us go on toward the north. Freedom awaits us."

Bruin was amazed at the change in his companion. He smiled, remembering the time he had wondered about making his escape with the hot-tempered little hunter. He had felt then that O-Tah-Wah's pride and courage would see him through.

Apparently he had been right. "Good!" he cried, covering the fire with earth. "We begin again."

* * * * *

Little Eyes studied the shining stream for a long while. He thought about the slaves they were following. He considered, too, the trick that had been played on him at the river the day before. Yet again he squinted down the gurgling, watery road to the north. He did not plan to be fooled another time! The dogs yelped and jumped about, yanking on the rawhide leashes that held them. "We cross the river," he ordered, and stepped toward the shallow stream. Several Mound Builders immediately began to question their chief.

"Why not follow the stream back northward until we strike their trail?" they asked. "We know which direction the slaves are traveling. Would they not take advantage of this creek? It leads that way." So sure were the warriors that they even dared question their chief's command!

Scornfully, Little Eyes stared them down. "How soon you forget the time we wasted earlier," he snarled. "Now we must be more clever than those we follow. If they are able to outwit us many more times, they will be out of our hunting grounds. Once this happens, their escape is certain!" Without another word, the crafty chief crossed the stream. It was but a matter of minutes until the dogs picked up the fresh trail on the west bank. Little Eyes sneered at his warriors in triumph as the dogs set up a wild racket. The trail was hot now, and the plunging animals fairly dragged their keepers through the brush.

But Little Eyes was not smiling. Even though he had outsmarted the runaways this time, the chief was aware that they were not yet caught. As he trotted along behind the trackers, every thought concentrated upon the hated men somewhere ahead of him. If Little Eyes could bring even some of the slaves back to the village, there was a good chance that he could take Cotauna's place as the highest ruler of the tribe. It had taken a long time for the villagers to forget the way Little Eyes had been fooled by the trader Turtle Shell. Little Eyes could not afford to be laughed at again! He ran harder, nearly passing the dogs themselves in his eagerness to close the distance between himself and his foes.

* * * * *

O-Tah-Wah was keeping up well, for the rest had given him new energy. Also, the young hunter had a plan. The plan gave him courage, and courage provided strength.

The air was growing rapidly warmer now, and for the first time, the two men noticed the heavy clouds that filled the sky above them. There was a feeling in the wind that both of them recognized. Winter was dying, and the clouds might hold rain. Rain would wash away tracks and blot out a man's scent on the earth. Rain would slow their pursuers and confuse the dogs. O-Tah-Wah prayed fervently to the Great Spirit for rain. Not for himself did he ask, but for the sake of his friend, Bruin.

Bruin was leading now, breaking trail through a tangle of high weeds that choked a small ravine. On either side of the gully, steep hills slanted sharply down upon them. O-Tah-Wah caught his breath as he glanced around. It was perfect! "Wait," he shouted at Bruin's broad back. "I must speak with you a moment."

Bruin stared at his friend in alarm. He hoped it was not another muscle cramp. It was too early to be certain, but the giant felt that they were now nearing the northern borders of the

Mound Builder hunting grounds. If the rains came and O-Tah-Wah's legs held out for just a little longer, they might actually make it! He was saving this information, however, in case O-Tah-Wah needed a moment of final encouragement.

"This is as far as I go!" O-Tah-Wah's arms were folded across his heaving chest, and it was very plain that he meant every word. Bruin tried to argue, but it was no use. "You know as well as I do that I cannot travel fast enough. If you wait for me, we shall both be captured. Therefore, I intend to stay here in this ravine. You must go on as fast as possible. When the Flatheads arrive, I shall hold them off as long as I can. Leave your weapons with me and run as you have never run before!"

Bruin did not know what to do. They were wasting precious minutes here. Suddenly, they both heard a sound that made the decision for them. The barking of a dog, faint but unmistakable, floated down the wind toward the slaves.

O-Tah-Wah began to speak. He was hurrying, for there was no time to lose. "I want to thank you," he began, "for being a friend to one who has known little of friendship." He drew a deep breath to continue but stopped with his mouth wide open. Bruin seemed hardly to be listening. The giant was too busy arranging his weapons and clothing for his final dash to freedom. O-Tah-Wah closed his mouth without saying any of the things he had planned. He stood in stunned silence, staring numbly at the man whom he had thought was his friend. Bruin only grinned his peculiar, ugly smile. The big slave did not leave his weapons at all, but after a quick slap on the smaller man's back, simply turned and trotted off. O-Tah-Wah stood for several moments staring at the bushes where Bruin had disappeared.

The first drops of rain began to fall at that moment. The barking could be heard again, too, and O-Tah-Wah, moving as one in a dream, slowly began preparing to defend himself.

The rain fell gently, but there was something in the look of the sky which hinted that much, much more was on the way. O-Tah-Wah shook himself violently, trying to clear his brain and throw off the despair that threatened to smother him. "So he is gone," he growled aloud. "I knew from the first that no one can truly be trusted. What does it matter, anyway? In a very short while I shall be dead. Or if I am unlucky, I shall be recaptured!" O-Tah-Wah thought again of Turtle Shell, and vowed that he, like the trader, would die here in this ravine rather than allow himself to be taken alive.

Struggling halfway up one of the steep, rocky banks, O-Tah-Wah selected a spot that gave him a good view of the entrance to the narrow gully. The location was ideal for an ambush. With good luck, he should be able to hold this position for a considerable time. "Run hard, Bruin my friend," he thought grimly as he settled himself behind a fallen tree trunk. "Do not worry, for I shall provide you with plenty of time!"

The Lazy One stuck out along the tree trunk, and as the small hunter looked at the leg, he began to notice something he had not felt for a long time. The old anger was returning! O-Tah-Wah almost welcomed the fury that was building rapidly within him.

Black eyes glittered under the dark, rain-plastered hair. Large drops were falling steadily now, and O-Tah-Wah squinted upward, letting the surprisingly warm rain fall straight into his face. There was no question about it—this was the first rain of spring.

O-Tah-Wah's hands were busy. All of his life, he had been a hunter. There would be a difference now, however, for he had never fired at a man before.

Four arrows were all he had. Fitting one onto the bowstring, he stuck the others in the earth nearby, as was his custom when preparing for rapid shooting. His clumsy, unfinished axe lay on the log before him. The flint knife remained in his belt. When he had placed a pinch of soil under his tongue, he was ready.

It took the dogs quite some time to track the runaways to the edge of the ravine. O-Tah-Wah's temper had quieted as he waited, but in its place a steely rage now gripped him. He tested the Mound Builder bow a few times. The smooth, steady draw was a delight. He felt savage pleasure in using the Flatheads' own weapons to hurt them.

An ugly, gray dog came snuffling up the slope. Its head was hanging, and O-Tah-Wah could tell that the animal was near exhaustion. The Mound Builder who followed looked worn out, too. The hidden slave watched from above as the dog repeatedly lost the trail, then found it again. Man and dog moved closer.

O-Tah-Wah raised himself slowly until his upper body was above the treetrunk. He pulled the sinew back, and when it touched his cheek, allowed the string to roll from the tips of his first and second finger. *Thwang*! The arrow seemed to fairly float down the slope to its target. The shot was low, but the shaft struck the man in the leg, knocking him down instantly. O-Tah-Wah laughed aloud as the dog, frightened by the yowling of its fallen keeper, spun around and dashed off into the brush, trailing the leash behind him.

Another Flathead came running toward his fallen comrade. O-Tah-Wah fired off two quick arrows, but both were misses. Before he could fire his final shaft, the Flathead had dragged his wounded companion out of sight. Knowing that the rest of the search party would soon be upon him, O-Tah-Wah drew his flint knife and gripped it between his teeth. At that moment, he saw a bow poised to fire near the point where the second Flathead had hidden. With hardly a thought, O-Tah-Wah drew his own bow and fired. A yell of pain told him his last arrow had found its mark!

For a few minutes, all was quiet. Then O-Tah-Wah saw three men and two dogs running toward him through the rain. They slipped and slid in the melting snow and the mud. Still they came nearer. O-Tah-Wah could only let them come, for he had no more arrows. Nothing could be done until they reached him. The brave hunter stood up then, pressing his back to a large rock. In one hand, his axe was ready. His knife was held low in the other hand. O-Tah-Wah knew that death was near, for he would never be able to last against three of the Flatheads.

All at once, a strange thing happened. One of the men scrambling toward him stumbled and fell headlong. The man lay very still, making no attempt to rise. The other men skidded to a stop and charged away toward the west. What could be happening? Then O-Tah-Wah saw a sight that brought a shout of joy to his lips. In a cleared space down the hill to his right, a giant form was bounding through the bushes, rushing straight at the Flatheads. "Bruin! It is Bruin!" the words burst out as in a flash he saw what had happened. Bruin had not tried to escape at all! He had circled back and hidden himself in order to attack from the side.

Even two Mound Builders and their dogs were no match for this whirlwind of strength and fury! Bruin came in fast, whirling the war club around his head and roaring like the animal whose name he bore. In a few seconds it was over.

Little Eyes' party was defeated. The chief himself, following a little way behind his warriors, had seen enough. Quietly, he turned and glided back the way he had come. Already, he was making up the story he would tell the villagers.

The heavens seemed to open then, and the rain poured down in great, drenching sheets. Laughing and shouting together, the two friends began to trot northward. There was no need to hurry now, for as the downpour continued, it washed their trail away so completely that neither man nor animal could have followed.

Nightfall found Bruin and O-Tah-Wah out of Mound Builder territory. Camped on a small knoll near a creek, they shared a roasted muskrat that Bruin had killed with a lucky throw of his war club. Bruin reached across the small fire and gripped his friend's forearm. "We must remain friends always," he said, "and wherever we go, we will tell the story of our escape from the Mound Builders."

— Epilogue —

O-Tah-Wah and Bruin did remain friends, and 22 years passed so quickly that O-Tah-Wah shook his head in wonder as he thought of it. His hair was now gray, and his three sons and daughters were nearly grown.

A loon laughed its way down the sweeping river that ran by the camp. "O-Tah-Wah's River," it was called by the tribes near-by. A short distance downstream, Bruin's lodge could be seen, nestling in a grove of small pines.

From this humble beginning would rise a great nation, one that would father wise and powerful chiefs, women kind and good, and many, many hunters and warriors of skill and courage. They would all be told the legend of their first chief, O-Tah-Wah.

The Ottawa Tribe was born!

THE AUTHOR

Lloyd Harnishfeger is an educator whose hobby is the study of life in prehistoric North America. His large personal collection of Indian relics, many of them found in a river valley near his home town, includes artifacts that are more than 4,000 years old. *Prisoner of the Mound Builders* and an earlier book, *Hunters of the Black Swamp*, reflect Mr. Harnishfeger's special interest in American prehistory and the special knowledge that he brings to the subject. Mr. Harnishfeger is a junior high school supervisor in the school system of Putnam County, Ohio. He lives in Pandora, Ohio, with his wife and daughter.